"Mark my words: Esau McCaulley is the brightest theological mind of this generation. *Reading While Black* is the oasis in the current Christian academic desert. As a professor, I can't wait to assign it, and as a pastor, I can't wait to employ it for discipleship. The Black student of the Bible instinctively knows the inherent risk of oversold lies and cultural mishaps at the intersection of our race and the reading of Scripture. In this work, we have a new light to walk the path straight."

Charlie Dates, senior pastor of Progressive Baptist Church, Chicago

"What does the Bible have to say to Black Christians seeking justice? By looking at well-known, overlooked, underinterpreted, and misinterpreted texts, Esau McCaulley tells us that a faithful reading of Scripture as the Word of God summons Black Christians (and others) to a cluster of practices. These include naming and protesting evil, expressing anger, and pursuing freedom and justice, but also promoting reconciliation, practicing forgiveness, and living in hope—all as aspects of proclaiming the gospel of the God revealed in Jesus. An important book."

Michael J. Gorman, Raymond E. Brown Chair in Biblical Studies and Theology at St. Mary's Seminary and University, Baltimore

"I don't know if I realized how much I needed this book until it landed in my hands. *Reading While Black* is scholarly yet reads clearly, communicating what many Black Christians have been saying for decades. Everyone would do well to listen up, lest they miss God in the process."

Jackie Hill-Perry, author of *Gay Girl, Good God*

"*Reading While Black* makes clear how the Scriptures, rightly read, are the source of Black justice and liberation, and how an orthodox belief in the authority of the Bible bolsters the dignity and flourishing of people of color in America. Theologically profound yet eminently accessible, Fr. Esau McCaulley masterfully weaves a dense and gorgeous tapestry of his personal narrative, insight into the Black church and American culture, and careful exegesis. I cannot think of a more relevant, pressing, helpful, and hopeful book for our contemporary moment."

Tish Harrison Warren, Anglican priest and author of *Liturgy of the Ordinary*

"Esau McCaulley's voice is one we urgently need to hear. This book is prophetic, biblical, measured, wise, friendly, and well-reasoned—and thus all the more hard-hitting. A powerful word for our times."

N. T. Wright, senior research fellow at Wycliffe Hall, Oxford

"This is a book for theologians who hope to play outside the trite sandboxes of their seminaries and for the practitioners who find themselves in need of a Black lexicon. McCaulley's anecdotes, definitions, and propositions are timely for a society that is desperate to reclaim dignity in the 'colorless' constructs that European Christianity built."

Sho Baraka, artist and cofounder of the AND Campaign

"In *Reading While Black*, Esau McCaulley is unapologetically Black, Christian, and committed to reading the Bible as Scripture and as relevant to the experience of Black folks. McCaulley demonstrates how the intuition and habits of Black biblical interpretation and the Black ecclesial tradition can help all readers connect the Bible and theology with the pressing issues of the day. Those who grab hold of this book and wrestle with it will be blessed."

Janette H. Ok, associate professor of New Testament at Fuller Theological Seminary

"In *Reading While Black*, Dr. Esau McCaulley honors the beautifully rich triumvirate of doxology, orthodoxy, and orthopraxy, which has always had its home in the Black Christian tradition."

Ekemini Uwan, writer and cohost of Truth's Table podcast

"In *Reading While Black*, McCaulley gives us more than a theoretical methodology; he demonstrates how we can approach and apply texts—even ones that were previously used against us—without jettisoning our faith or succumbing to oppressive readings. *Reading While Black* is a welcome addition to the study of African American hermeneutics."

Dennis R. Edwards, associate professor of New Testament at North Park University

"I'm extremely grateful to have a voice in my time to speak with nuance, grace, and cultural awareness. Esau has given us a healthy marriage for understanding theology and blackness. This is a must-read!"

Lecrae, hip hop recording artist

"It is enlightening, moving, and galvanizing to overhear these notes of appreciation and reciprocated encouragement from a son of the Black church to the Black ecclesial interpreters who nurtured and continue to nourish him. From here on out, this book will be required reading in any course on biblical hermeneutics that I teach."

Wesley Hill, associate professor of biblical studies, Trinity School for Ministry

"*Reading While Black* is a unique and successful blend of biblical hermeneutics, autobiography, black history and spirituality, incisive cultural commentary on race matters in America, and insightful exegesis of select New Testament texts."

Nijay K. Gupta, professor of New Testament at Northern Seminary

"In *Reading While Black*, Rev. Dr. Esau McCaulley puts in bold relief before us the historic and present concerns of the African American community. With sound exegetical method, deep cultural insight, and skillful application he brings us into the heart of God on these issues. Know, however, that this is not just a book for Black people. Far from it. Anyone who desires to engage these questions with gospel hope should take up and read."

Irwyn L. Ince Jr., author of *The Beautiful Community*

"Dr. Esau McCaulley combines his training in New Testament scholarship with his love for the Black church tradition. The result of his labor is a fresh and accessible contribution to African American reception history of the Bible."

Jarvis J. Williams, associate professor of New Testament interpretation at the Southern Baptist Theological Seminary

"This is a must-read for pastors, college students, seminarians, and anyone interested in learning about how African American Bible interpretation can speak a word of hope to us in our day. It addresses questions Black Christians have been asking about issues such as policing, Black identity, political protest, and the pursuit of justice from a perspective that takes the Bible and its critics seriously."

Lisa Fields, founder and president of the Jude 3 Project

"*Reading While Black* will provide you with insights into the gospel that will transform your life, regardless of your ethnicity. The horizons of your spiritual formation will expand as a result of reading this book; you will read and return to it over and over."

Derwin L. Gray, author of *The Good Life: What Jesus Teaches About Finding True Happiness*

"Esau McCaulley rightfully insists that reading the Bible well does not mean abandoning one's ethnicity. Instead, one must read precisely from one's location while at the same time allowing the Bible to broaden our horizons. This is a book that African American pastors and scholars need to consider carefully. In fact, it is a book that church leaders from every race in North America need to ponder."

Osvaldo Padilla, professor of divinity at Beeson Divinity School

READING WHILE BLACK

AFRICAN AMERICAN
BIBLICAL INTERPRETATION
AS AN EXERCISE IN HOPE

ESAU McCAULLEY

iVp
Academic

An imprint of InterVarsity Press
Downers Grove, Illinois

InterVarsity Press
P.O. Box 1400, Downers Grove, IL 60515-1426
ivpress.com
email@ivpress.com

InterVarsity Press® is the book-publishing division of InterVarsity Christian Fellowship/USA®, a movement of students and faculty active on campus at hundreds of universities, colleges, and schools of nursing in the United States of America, and a member movement of the International Fellowship of Evangelical Students. For information about local and regional activities, visit intervarsity.org.

Scripture quotations, unless otherwise noted, are from the New Revised Standard Version of the Bible, copyright 1989 by the Division of Christian Education of the National Council of the Churches of Christ in the USA. Used by permission. All rights reserved.

Cover design and image composite: David Fassett
Interior design: Jeanna Wiggins
Images: man with folded hands: © caracterdesign / E+ / Getty Images
   paper texture: © Matthieu Tuffet / iStock / Getty Images Plus
   open Bible: © TokenPhoto / E+ / Getty Images

ISBN 978-0-8308-5486-8 (print)
ISBN 978-0-8308-5487-5 (digital)

Printed in the United States of America ♾

InterVarsity Press is committed to ecological stewardship and to the conservation of natural resources in all our operations. This book was printed using sustainably sourced paper.

Library of Congress Cataloging-in-Publication Data

A catalog record for this book is available from the Library of Congress.

P   25   24   23   22   21   20   19   18   17   16   15   14   13   12   11   10   9   8   7   6   5   4   3   2

Y   41   40   39   38   37   36   35   34   33   32   31   30   29   28   27   26   25   24   23   22   21   20

THIS BOOK IS DEDICATED
TO THE MEMORY OF

Esau McCaulley Sr.

who died before he ever got to see

a book bearing our name in print.

Whatever else I am,

I will always remain your son.

CONTENTS

Acknowledgments   ix

1 The South Got Somethin' to Say   1
Making Space for Black Ecclesial Interpretation

2 Freedom Is No Fear   25
The New Testament and a Theology of Policing

3 Tired Feet, Rested Souls   47
The New Testament and the Political Witness of the Church

4 Reading While Black   71
The Bible and the Pursuit of Justice

5 Black and Proud   96
The Bible and Black Identity

6 What Shall We Do with This Rage?   118
The Bible and Black Anger

7 The Freedom of the Slaves   137
Pennington's Triumph

Conclusion: *An Exercise in Hope*   164

Bonus Track: *Further Notes on the Development of Black Ecclesial Interpretation*   168

Discussion Guide   185

Bibliography   187

Author Index   195

Scripture Index   197

ACKNOWLEDGMENTS

THIS BOOK WOULD HAVE BEEN impossible without the help of friends, family, and colleagues.

To my mother, Laurie, thank you for dragging us to church even when we didn't want to go and instilling in us a God-given hope for better things. This book is as much yours as it is mine. To my siblings—Latasha, Marketha, and Brandon—thank you for loving your brother even when I didn't make it easy.

To my wife, Mandy, thank you for everything.

To Luke, Clare, Peter, and Miriam, my desire is that when times get difficult you will remember to read the texts of the Old and New Testament and find in them a source of hope like our ancestors did. If you ever forget what that hope looks like, I pray this book will guide you.

To Lisa Fields of the Jude 3 project, thank you for reminding me of the community to which I am responsible. To Tish Harrison Warren, thank you for helping me remember that writing can and should be beautiful. Thank you to Charlie Dates for modeling what faithful black church preaching and pastoring should look like, and to Justin Giboney of the AND Campaign for helping me recall that faithful advocacy is still possible.

To N. T. Wright, thank you for believing in me as a doctoral student and encouraging me to find my own way in the academy.

To the faculty, staff, and students of Northeastern Seminary and now Wheaton College, I am grateful for the encouragement and conversations along the way.

Thank you to Anna Gissing and the people of InterVarsity Press for believing in the importance of this project. Anna, you deserve a medal for all the texts, phone calls, and emails that you received. I'll be better next time. (Well, I probably won't.)

ONE

THE SOUTH GOT
SOMETHIN' TO SAY

MAKING SPACE FOR BLACK
ECCLESIAL INTERPRETATION

■ ■ ■

*But just as we have the same spirit of faith
that is in accordance with scripture—"I believed, and
so I spoke"—we also believe, and so we speak.*

2 CORINTHIANS 4:13

*But it's like this, though. . . . I'm tired of folks—you know what
I'm sayin'—closed minded folks. It's like we got a demo tape
and don't nobody wanna hear it. But it's like this.
The South got somethin' to say.*

ANDRÉ 3000

MY MOTHER TRIED HER BEST to immerse her children in the gospel.
Most Sundays there was no question where we would be. The Mc-
Caulleys would be safely ensconced in our pew at Union Hill Prim-
itive Baptist church in Huntsville, Alabama, from 10:00 a.m. until

the Spirit had finished his work. There was, however, always a chance that my mother would be too tired from working at the Chrysler factory to drag her four unruly children to the house of the Lord. To encourage this fatigue to do *its work,* we would stay in our rooms as quiet as church mice hoping not to rouse her from her slumber. The signal that our plan had failed was the sound of Mahalia Jackson on the radio. Once Mahalia started in on "Amazing Grace," the jig was up.

Our home knew Gospel music. In addition to Mahalia we received a steady stream of Shirley Caesar telling us to hold her mule and James Cleveland reminding us that he didn't feel no ways tired. Gospel music filled our home and shaped our imaginations even when we rebelled against it.

The second witness continually brought to bear upon the hopes and dreams of her four children was the large King James Bible that lived on a shelf in the living room. The King functioned more like a talisman than a book to be read. Whenever my mother wanted to wring the truth out of us, she would have us place our hands on the KJV and declare that what we had told her was the truth. Only the most brazen of sinners among us would dare speak falsehood in the presence of mom, Jesus, and King James. We also watched Christian cartoons (*Superbook*) and went to midweek Bible studies and as many Vacation Bible Schools as we could manage. The Scriptures were everywhere.

But I was also a child of my environment. I was a southern Black boy from Alabama in love with hip hop. As soon as my mother pressed pause on Mahalia, I pressed play on Southern hip hop. OutKast, Goodie Mob, and the bass coming out of Miami boomed in the Delta 88 that I drove to and from the schools and parties of Northwest Huntsville. That music also helped me interpret the world that seemed to have its foot on the neck of Black and Brown bodies in my city.

Put simply, I knew the Lord and the culture. Both engaged in an endless battle for my affections. I loved hip hop because sometimes it felt as if only the rappers truly understood what it was like to experience the heady mix of danger, drama, and temptation that marked Black life in the South. They spoke of the drugs, the violence, the encounters with the police—and even God. They did not so much offer solutions as much as they reflected on the life forced on them. But I also loved my mother's Gospel music because it filled me with hope, and it connected me to something old and immovable. If hip hop tended toward nihilism and utilitarian ethics (the game is the game so we do what we must to survive), then my mother's music, rooted in biblical texts and ideas, offered a vision of something bigger and wider. The struggle I speak of is not merely between two genres of music. I am referring to the struggle between Black nihilism and Black hope. I am speaking of the ways in which the Christian tradition fights for and makes room for hope in a world that tempts us toward despair. I contend that a key element in this fight for hope in our community has been the practice of Bible reading and interpretation coming out of the Black church, what I am calling Black ecclesial interpretation.

The nineties were a time of hip hop controversy with the two coasts—East and West—at war with one another. A record company called Death Row, which specialized in the gangster rap music that chronicled life on the streets of California, led the way out West. Bad Boy records, on the East coast, represented a tradition that valued lyrical dexterity and Black celebration. The struggle at the center of their conflict was the nature of rap music itself. What was the correct demeanor, tone, and focus?

The brewing hostility came to a head in 1995 at the second annual *Source* awards. This gathering was the celebratory event of a magazine that was the arbiter of Black hip hop culture in the 1990s. In 1995, it was held in New York. Thus, the crowd was decidedly in favor of all things East. Whenever a West Coast artist won, the boos came in full force. Eventually, the show made its way to the award for the best new artist. Neither an East Coast or West Coast artist won. Instead, OutKast, a group from the South with no particular ties to either coast, emerged victorious. But the times were what the times were, and since they weren't from the East, they were jeered at what should have been their moment of victory.

In response, André 3000, the more outlandish member of the duo, stood before the crowd and spoke the quote that opened this chapter:

> But it's like this, though. . . . I'm tired of folks—you know what I'm sayin'—closed minded folks. It's like we got a demo tape and don't nobody wanna hear it. But it's like this. The South got somethin' to say.[1]

André declared that he would not apologize for being Southern, Black, and different. While he appreciated what the West and East had to offer to the culture, the South was a third thing worthy of respect in its own right. The pressure and the criticism, then, didn't break them. It sent them back to the studio. The result was an album titled *Aquemini*, recognized by many as one of the most influential hip hop records ever written. It remains a strange album, unapologetically Southern, but also influenced by elements of the East and the West. Freed from the strictures of coastal allegiance, they had space to be creative. I have often thought that Black ecclesial interpreters need the freedom to be *Aquemini*, some other thing that is truly our own.

What do I mean when I refer to Black ecclesial interpreters? I have in mind Black scholars and pastors formed by the faith found in the

---

[1]This story is retold in *ATL: The Untold Story of Atlanta's Rise in the Rap Game*, a VH1 documentary released in 2014.

foundational and ongoing doctrinal commitments, sermons, public witness, and ethos of the Black church. For a variety of reasons, this ecclesial tradition rarely appears in print. It lives in the pulpits, sermon manuscripts, CDs, tape ministries, and videos of the African American Christian tradition.

Let's be clear. The Black Christian tradition is not and has never been a monolith, but it is fair to say that the Black church tradition is largely orthodox in its theology in the sense that it holds to many of the things that all Christians have generally believed. This orthodoxy is reflected in the statements of faith of three of the larger Black denominations: the National Baptist Convention, the Church of God in Christ (COGIC), and African Methodist Episcopal Church (AME).[2] Nonetheless, Black theologians and writers who share these views sometimes find themselves in the place of OutKast during the *Source* awards. We are thrust into the middle of a battle between white progressives and white evangelicals, feeling alienated in different ways from both. When we turn our eyes to our African American progressive sisters and brothers, we nod our head in agreement on many issues. Other times we experience a strange feeling of dissonance, one of being at home and away from home. Therefore, we receive criticism from all sides for being something different, a fourth thing.[3] I am calling this fourth thing Black ecclesial theology and its method Black ecclesial interpretation. I am not proposing a new idea or method but attempting to articulate and apply a practice that already exists.

---

[2]See the Church of God in Christ statement of faith at www.cogic.org/about-company /statement-of-faith. The statement from the National Baptists can be found at www .nationalbaptist.com/about-nbc/what-we-believe. The beliefs of the African Methodist Episcopal church can be found at www.ame-church.com/our-church/our-beliefs.

[3]As will be clear in the next chapter, I do not contend that the Black progressive tradition exists outside of the Black church. They are one manifestation of it. They remain part of a constant conversation without our communities about the nature of Black faith.

I want to make a case that this fourth thing, this unapologetically Black and orthodox reading of the Bible can speak a relevant word to Black Christians today. I want to contend that the best instincts of the Black church tradition—its public advocacy for justice, its affirmation of the worth of Black bodies and souls, its vision of a multiethnic community of faith—can be embodied by those who stand at the center of this tradition. This is a work against the cynicism of some who doubt that the Bible has something to say; it is a work contending for hope.

To explain how I concluded that the Black ecclesial tradition has a word for our day, I would like to take you on something of a whirlwind tour of the exegetical communities that I have known. My discussion may appear to be anecdotal, but it is nonetheless rooted in a long engagement with scholars and pastors from each tradition. A full and nuanced discussion would occupy the entire book, but I do hope, even when I am critical, to have avoided caricature. This introduction will set the stage for the more constructive work that will occupy the majority of this book.

PROGRESSIVES, EVANGELICALS, AND BLACK STUDENTS

The first day of college introduced me to the white classroom. Before then everything had been Black: church, neighborhood, school, and sports teams. My university, by contrast, felt like it was 98 percent white. I knew when I agreed to attend that it was largely white. The recruiters, however, told me that the cultural discomfort was a small price to pay for a quality education. What did I know? I was a teenager trying my best to navigate the unfamiliar world of higher education.

I decided to double major in history and religion because those two topics, the history of my people and my Christian faith, stood at the center of my identity. I had read on my own about the middle passage, slavery, the Civil War, Reconstruction, the Harlem Renaissance, the Civil Rights Movement, and the crack epidemic. But I wanted to know more. I needed to know how we got to where we were, and then discern how the lessons of history might help me chart a way forward. More urgently, I thought it was a story that needed telling. But I was also a Christian having been raised to love Jesus and the Scriptures. I wanted to go beyond simple answers to difficult questions. I wanted to be challenged and stretched to understand my beliefs as well as those of others. Rather than choose, I decided to pursue the best of both worlds. I would study the Bible and history. But by the end of my second year of college, only one of those majors would remain.

Every devout student who experiences higher biblical criticism for the first time is inevitably a bit bewildered. Things that were once simple become much more complicated. How do we reconcile the two creation accounts in Genesis? How do we deal with differences in the Gospels? How do we bring Paul and James into conversation with one another in a way that allows both voices to be heard? What should we do with the book of Revelation? What about the violence in the Old and New Testaments and the passages that make our ears tingle?

Learning about the Bible changes our faith (and hopefully it matures and deepens it). Much depends on what the professor in the class attempts to do. He or she is not our pastor; it is not their job to be safe. Some skirt the problems saying that difficulties are not so difficult. Others face those problems head on and chart a different path through them to the other side. Some leave the students to wrestle with these questions on their own. Others still have a particular agenda: their goal is deconstruction.

When I walked into my first Bible class, I unknowingly entered the hundred years' war between white evangelicals and white mainline Protestants. My professors displayed sympathy for the latter. Their goal was to rid their students of the white fundamentalism that they believed was the cause of every ill that beset the South. A better South was the progressive South of the white mainline church. It seems that in their minds, a progressive South was only possible when we rejected the centrality of the Bible for something more *fundamental*, namely the white mainline Protestant consensus on politics, economics, and religion. I got the feeling that they believed that "the older stories" and "the older gods" were profitable as tales to spur reflection, but could not compete with the new insights bequeathed to us by the latest declarations of Western intellectuals. In this story, Black students do not really enter in as *actors*. We are acted upon, our suffering functioning as examples of the evils of white fundamentalism.

My professors had a point. One does not have to dig very far into history to see that fundamentalist Christians in the South (and the North) have indeed inflicted untold harm on Black people. They have used the Bible as justification for their sins, personal and corporate. But there is a second testimony possibly more important than the first. That is the testimony of Black Christians who saw in *that same Bible* the basis for their dignity and hope in a culture that often denied them both. In my professor's attempt to take the Bible away from the fundamentalists, he also robbed the Black Christian of the rock on which they stood.[4]

There was something broken about this to me. If the Scriptures were fundamentally flawed and largely useless apart from mainline

---

[4]We will leave aside for the moment the fact that while I accept elements of higher criticism, I did not find all the arguments or conclusions of my professors compelling. To chronicle these differences, however, would be a different book.

revision of the text, then *Christianity is truly a white man's* religion. They were reconstructing it without my consent. Moreover, the form of this reconstructed religion bore the image of the twentieth-century European intellectual.

If the Bible needs to be rejected to free Black Christians, then such a view seems to entail that the fundamentalists had interpreted the Bible correctly. All the things that racists had done to us, then, had strong biblical warrant. My professor's victory felt too much like my mother's defeat. She had always told me that the racists were the poor interpreters and that we were reading correctly when we saw in biblical texts describing the worth of all people an affirmation of Black dignity. This entire debate had been crafted and carried on without any regard for the Black testimony. I was a casualty of someone else's war.

In the end this war was not terribly interesting to me, and I decided that I would focus my efforts on history. I dropped my religion major, not because it challenged my faith with hard questions, but because it didn't ask the *right hard questions.*[5] Nonetheless, the questions raised in those classes set me on a journey that ironically enough would lead me back to the issues surrounding the Bible and its relationship to Black culture.

The other solution on offer at my university was the evangelical world that my professors and others told me to avoid. They warned me that the evangelicals were heirs to the fundamentalists and were not to be trusted. At first all was well. Evangelicals spoke about the Bible in a way that had points of connection with the Black church. Their emphasis on the Scriptures reminded me of the tradition that formed me. Given that *evangelical* means different things to different people, it is important to clarify what I mean by the term.

---

[5]See the chapter on Black rage as an example of the questions I have in mind.

Historian David Bebbington's definition has been accepted by many as a good starting point. He outlines four characteristics:

- Conversionism: the belief that lives need to be transformed through a "born-again" experience and a lifelong process of following Jesus.

- Activism: the expression and demonstration of the gospel in missionary and social reform efforts.

- Biblicism: a high regard for and obedience to the Bible as the ultimate authority.

- Crucicentrism: a stress on the sacrifice of Jesus Christ on the cross as making possible the redemption of humanity.[6]

It is common knowledge that when it comes to beliefs about the Bible and Christian theology more generally, evangelicals and Black churches have much in common.[7] Very few Black churches would have a problem with what is included in this list. The problem is what is left out.

My sojourn among the evangelicals began after I dropped my religion major to focus on history, especially the history of African Americans in the United States. Upon graduation, I decided to return to the study of theology and pursue a Master of Divinity at an evangelical seminary. I made this decision because I was still struggling to decide between theological research and Black history and culture. I didn't yet realize that this was a false choice.

---

[6]David Bebbington, *Evangelicalism in Modern Britain: A History from the 1730s to the 1980s* (London: Routledge, 1989), 1-17. See also Mark Noll, *The Rise of Evangelicalism* (Downers Grove, IL: IVP Academic, 2003), 17-20.

[7]Pew Research found that 59 percent of Black Protestants and 57 percent of evangelicals believe that the Bible is the Word of God and should be interpreted "literally." See "Members of the Historically Black Protestant Tradition Who Identify as Black," Pew Research Forum, accessed February 26, 2020, www.pewforum.org/religious-landscape-study /racial-and-ethnic-composition/Black/religious-tradition/historically-Black-protestant.

The more time I spent among evangelicals, the more I realized that those spaces can subtly and not subtly breed a certain disdain for what they see as the "uncouthness" of Black culture. We were told that our churches weren't sound theologically because our clergy did not always speak the language of the academy. In my evangelical seminary almost all the authors we read were white men. It was as if all the important conversations about the Bible began when the Germans started to take the text apart, and the Bible lay in tatters until the evangelicals came to put it back together again. I learned the contours of the debate between British evangelicals and German liberals. It seemed that whatever was going on among Black Christians had little to do with real biblical interpretation. I swam in this disdain, and even when I rejected it vocally, the doubt seeped into my subconscious.

Eventually I started to notice a few things. While I was at home with much of the theology in evangelicalism, there were real disconnects. First, there was the portrayal of the Black church in these circles. I was told that the social gospel had corrupted Black Christianity. Rather than placing my hope there, I should look to the golden age of theology, either at the early years of this country or during the postwar boom of American Protestantism. But the historian in me couldn't help but realize that these apexes of theological faithfulness coincided with nadirs of Black freedom.

I learned that too often alongside the four pillars of evangelicalism outlined above there were unspoken fifth and sixth pillars. These are a general agreement on a certain reading of American history that downplayed injustice and a gentlemen's agreement to remain largely silent on current issues of racism and systemic injustice. How could I exist comfortably in a tradition that too often valorizes a period of time when my people couldn't buy homes in the neighborhoods that they wanted or attend the schools that their skills gave them access to? How could I accept a place in a community if the cost for a seat at the table was silence?

My struggle was more than different readings of American history and issues of justice. I had difficulty with how the Bible *functioned* in parts of evangelicalism. For many, the Bible had been reduced to the arena on which we fought an endless war about the finer points of Paul's doctrine of justification. True scholars were those who could articulate the latest twists and turns in a debate that has raged since the Reformation. Yes, the question of our standing before God is important, vitally important (I laud the great emphases of the Reformation). But I wondered what the Bible had to say about how we might live as Christians and citizens of God's kingdom. I was told that the Bible says we must defend the sanctity of life, the authority of the government (including the military and the police), and religious freedom. Again, each of these questions are important. I am pro-life. I am not an anarchist. But what about the exploitation of my people? What about our suffering, our struggle? Where does the Bible address the hopes of Black folks, and why is this question not pressing in a community that has historically been alienated from Black Christians?

I read biblical commentaries that displayed little concern for how biblical texts speak to the experiences of Black believers. When there was an attempt to provide practical applications to texts, these applications were too often designed for white middle-class Christians. Others decided not to apply the text at all. Instead scholars simply described the Jewish and Christian world of the first century. To me, it was a sign of privilege to imprison Paul and Jesus in the first century. For Paul, his Scriptures (the Old Testament) were a fire that leaped the gap and spoke a word to his ethnically mixed churches about the nature of their life together. What an audacious thought! The Black pastors I knew had the same audacity to think that texts of the New Testament spoke directly to the issues facing Black Christians. They were part of a long history of Black interpreters who felt the same. Therefore, while I appreciated the doctrinal emphasis on Scripture within evangelicalism, I needed more to feel whole and complete as a Christian. I felt a strong call to dig deep into the roots of the Black Christian tradition to help me navigate the complexities of Black existence in the United States.

ROOTING FOR EVERYBODY BLACK: A STOP ALONG THE WAY

On the red carpet before the 2017 Emmys, *Variety* magazine interviewed African American writer, director, producer, and actor Issa Rae. They asked her who she was rooting for to win an award. She said that she was rooting for everyone Black. Why did she say this? Did she hate all non-Black nominees? No. Because when there are so few Blacks in Hollywood every Black victory becomes a matter of celebration.

What did I do in a world in which so few Black voices are prominent and the questions of my people were ignored? I began to look for anybody Black. I began to search for theologians who could help me make sense of what it means to be Black and Christian. For those who came up through schools like the ones that I attended that assigned so few Black and Brown voices, the journey of finding "somebody Black" was often a solitary one.

When I found African American theological voices in print, I was overjoyed to discover people who seemed to care about some of the same things that I cared about. The conversations in these works felt like the raw and honest talk that went on between my aunts and uncles at dinner tables where only "grown folks" were allowed. The more I read, the more I realized that not all my aunts and uncles were at the table, but a particular auntie or uncle that I knew well. Most Black writers that I encountered were from the progressive strand of the Black Christian tradition. I was happy to engage these authors, but I couldn't shake the feeling that voices were missing.

One more story. Midway through the writing of this chapter, I was invited to give a lecture on Black biblical interpretation to a group of COGIC pastors. I began by outlining much of the material covered so far. I spoke about the Black church of my youth, mainline Protestantism, Evangelicalism, and the Black progressive tradition. I had planned on discussing the strengths and weaknesses of each when a pastor stopped me in the middle of the lecture and asked what they were supposed to do. He said that he accepted my criticism of a complacent orthodoxy that doesn't advocate for the oppressed. But when he sends his clergy to colleges and seminaries that share his concern for the disinherited, too often that comes at the price of the theological beliefs that he holds dear. I was asked where one could go that shares their social concerns and takes seriously their belief that the Scriptures are God's Word to us for our good. Who could they read that combined both? They said it seemed like they needed to go to one source for theological analysis and another for social practice.

That conversation distilled for me the growing sense of unease with elements of the Black progressive enterprise. I could nod my head during some of the social analysis, but some Black progressives shared the same disdain for traditional belief that I had witnessed among my mainline professors. The main difference between Black and white progressives was that the former put the revision of Christian belief into direct conversation with the experiences of the Black community. For many of them a traditional understanding of the Christian faith limited the work of liberation.

They often saw the Bible as being as much a part of the problem as the solution.

To be fair, they often found great solace in the broad themes of the Bible. They knew the prophets and Jesus' own words about how the poor deserve dignity and are loved by God. It was true that insomuch as they spoke about these things they echoed a tradition that I knew, but other elements of the Christian story were changed and shifted in a way that I could not quite articulate. Moreover, I was told repeatedly that this was *Black theology*. I felt torn between what some Black theologians told me Black theology was, and my lived or ecclesial experience.

When Issa Rae said that she was rooting for everybody Black at the Emmys, she referred to everyone up for an award at that event. I am sure that we can all admit that some depictions of Black life in Hollywood written and directed by Black people are problematic. Few would counsel against discernment. I discovered that I too had to learn to read every one, even Black theologians, critically against the backdrop of a faith that I believed to be most consistent with the Scriptures.

Talking of reading critically is a slightly dangerous thing because Black traditional voices are often weaponized in evangelical spaces against Black progressive voices. Some Black progressives have theological ideas that trouble evangelicals. Rather than dismiss Black progressives directly and be accused of racism, evangelicals sometimes bring Black (theological) conservatives in to do that work.

To avoid the perception of being tokenized, the alternative for Black traditionalists is to avoid discussion of Black progressives altogether. But the problem is that there are places where a rigorous debate is necessary. They are places where we simply disagree.

In other words, there is a well-worn path of Black affirmation in white conservative spaces if one is willing to denigrate Black theology (and the Black church) full stop. But the converse also occurs, namely that white progressives have often weaponized Black progressive voices and depicted them as the totality of the Black Christian tradition for reasons that suit their own purposes, which have little to do with the actual concerns of Black Christians. What I am suggesting is an ongoing discussion among Black Christians where neither partner is presumed to be arguing in bad faith or merely puppeting white voices.

I am still rooting for Black theologians and biblical scholars. We need more voices not fewer, but that doesn't mean there isn't space for rigorous disagreement and debate about the nature, sources, and means of the Black interpretive enterprise.

THE METHOD THAT COMES OUT OF MY STRUGGLES

Nonetheless, my experiences with the Black progressive tradition finally sent me back to the sources with one question. What were the key elements of the early Black theological enterprise especially as it relates to the practice of Bible reading?[8]

The first ray of hope came from Frederick Douglass, whose words came to be something of a Balm in Gilead. He said,

> What I have said respecting and against religion, I mean strictly to apply to the slaveholding religion of this land, and with no possible reference to Christianity proper; for, between the Christianity of this land, and the Christianity of Christ, I recognize the widest possible difference. . . . I love the pure, peaceable, and impartial Christianity of Christ: I therefore hate the corrupt, slaveholding, women-whipping, cradle-plundering, partial and hypocritical Christianity of this land.[9]

---

[8]For a more detailed discussion of what I found, see the bonus track on the development of the Black ecclesial method.
[9]Frederick Douglass, *The Life of an American Slave* (Boston: Anti-Slavery Office, 1845), 117.

Frederick then posits a distinction, not so much between Black Christianity and white, but between slaveholder religion and the Christianity of Jesus and the Bible. Black Christianity historically, I would come to understand, has claimed that white slave master readings of the Bible used to undergird white degradation of Black bodies were not merely one manifestation of Christianity to be contrasted with another. Instead they said that such a reading was wrong. Enslaved Black people, even those who remained illiterate, in effect questioned white exegesis.

It is also well known that these enslaved persons, over against their masters' wishes, viewed events like God's redemption of Israel from slavery as paradigmatic for their understanding of God's character. They claimed that God is fundamentally a liberator. The character of Jesus, who though innocent suffered unjustly at the hands of an empire, resonated on a deep level with the plight of the enslaved Black person. This focus on God as liberator stood in stark contrast to the focus of the slave masters who emphasized God's desire for a social order with white masters at the top and enslaved Black people at the bottom. But the story doesn't stop there. Alongside the story of the God of the exodus is the God of Leviticus, who calls his people to a holiness of life. The formerly enslaved managed to celebrate both their physical liberation and their spiritual transformation, which came as a result of their encounter with the God of the Old and New Testaments.

The social location of enslaved persons caused them to read the Bible differently. This unabashedly *located* reading has marked African American interpretation since. Did this social location mean Blacks rejected biblical texts that did not match their understanding of God? Did Blacks create a canon within a canon?

The story is often told of Howard Thurman's experience of reading the Bible for his grandmother, a former slave. Rather than have him read the entire Bible, she omitted sections of Paul's letters. At first he did not question this practice. Later he works up the courage to ask her why she avoids Paul:

> "During the days of slavery," she said, "the master's minister would occasionally hold services for the slaves. Old man McGhee was so mean that he would not let a Negro minister preach to his slaves. Always the white minister used as his text something from Paul. At least three or four times a year he used as a text: 'Slaves, be obedient to them that are your masters . . . as unto Christ.' Then he would go on to show how it was God's will that we were slaves and how, if we were good and happy slaves, God would bless us. I promised my Maker that if I ever learned to read and if freedom ever came, I would not read that part of the Bible."[10]

This idea has even led some to call enslaved people the first to recognize the limits of the Scriptures. They knew that God was a God of freedom and any biblical text that spoke differently must be resisted. While I agree that the enslaved people resisted any attempt to use the Bible to justify slavery, I think that such a view may concede too much. It implies that the slave masters themselves did not have a canon within a canon. Notice that the slave master whenever he had Paul read focused on a few texts. Whatever we might say of the Pauline slave texts, few would argue that Paul's thoughts on slavery stand at the center of his theological world. Furthermore, it is also interesting to note that other portions of Paul's letters such as Galatians 3:28 were not popular among slave masters.

Furthermore, we know that they avoided those Old Testament passages that spoke of God as liberator of the enslaved. It is not the case that Blacks uniquely emphasized certain passages and read other Scriptures in light of them; what was unique was *what* enslaved

---

[10]Howard Thurman, *Jesus and the Disinherited* (Boston: Beacon Press, 1976), 30.

Black people emphasized. They emphasized God as the liberator and humankind as one family united under the rule of Christ whose death for sins reconciles us to God. To put it more pointedly, I contend that the enslaved reading of the exodus as paradigmatic for understanding God's character was more faithful to the biblical text than those who began with the Pauline slave passages.

But the problem is deeper still. The slave masters agreed that passages such as 1 Timothy 6:1-3 had a limited application. They did not apply to white Christians. Therefore, as it relates to the applicability of the slave passages to their wives and children, they would agree that the gospel liberates *them* from the specter of slavery. However, they concocted a theory of the subhumanity of Africans to justify their mistreatment. Yet the biblical interpretation of enslaved persons rejected this categorization of Blacks as less than human, and thereby claimed the same exemption from slavery that applied to the rest of God's creation.

Therefore, I contend that the enslaved person's biblical interpretation, which gave birth to early Black biblical interpretation, was *canonical* from its inception. It placed Scripture's dominant themes in conversation with the hopes and dreams of Black folks. It was also unabashedly *theological*, in that particular texts were read in light of their doctrine of God, their beliefs about humanity (anthropology) and their understanding of salvation (soteriology).

It is true that Blacks were drawn to Christianity because elements of the Old Testament story and elements of Jesus' life coincided with their own experience. These factors cannot be denied, but just as their context spoke to the Bible, the Bible, as the Word of God, spoke back. It expanded their understanding of their plight and their relationship to the wider human story. As I began to reflect on what I was reading and seeing in these primary sources, the beginning of what I call the Black ecclesial instinct or method became clear.

I propose that dialogue, rooted in core theological principles, between the Black experience and the Bible has been the model and needs to be carried forward into our day. This means that it is laudable to engage in what Brian Blount, noted New Testament scholar, called an "academically unorthodox experiment" of asking questions of the text that grow out the reality of being Black in America.[11]

This is not unique to Black Christians. Blount again says that "Euro-American scholars, ministers, and lay folk . . . have, over the centuries, used their economic, academic, religious, and political dominance to create the illusion that the Bible, read through their experience, is the Bible read correctly."[12] Stated differently, everybody has been reading the Bible from their locations, but we are honest about it. What makes Black interpretation Black, then, are the collective experiences, customs, and habits of Black people in this country.

But the dialogue goes both ways. If our experiences pose particular and unique questions to the Scriptures, then the Scriptures also pose unique questions to us. Although there are some experiences that are common to humanity, there are also some ways in which the Bible will pose particular challenges to African Americans. For example, the theme of forgiveness and the universal kinship of humanity is both a boon and a trial for Black Christians because of the historic and ongoing oppression of Black people in this country. Although I believe we must engage in a dialogue with the text, I acknowledge that ultimately the Word of God speaks the final word.

For those of us who want to continue to affirm the ongoing normative role of the Bible in the life of the church, it will not do to

---

[11]Brian K. Blount, *Then the Whisper Put on Flesh: New Testament Ethics in an African American Context* (Nashville: Abingdon Press, 2001), 16.
[12]Blount, *Then the Whisper Put on Flesh*, 15.

dismiss the concerns raised about the Bible from many quarters. The path forward is not a return to the naiveté of a previous generation, but a journeying through the hard questions while being informed by the roots of the tradition bequeathed to us. I propose instead that we adopt the posture of Jacob and refuse to let go of the text until it blesses us. Stated differently, we adopt a hermeneutic of trust in which we are patient with the text in the belief that when interpreted properly it will bring a blessing and not a curse. This means that we do the hard work of reading the text closely, attending to historical context, grammar, and structure.

My claim then is that Black biblical interpretation has been and can be

- unapologetically *canonical* and *theological.*
- socially located, in that it clearly arises out of the particular *context* of Black Americans.
- willing to *listen* to the ways in which the Scriptures themselves respond to and redirect Black issues and concerns.
- willing to exercise *patience* with the text trusting that a careful and sympathetic reading of the text brings a blessing.
- willing to listen to and enter into dialogue with Black and white critiques of the Bible in the hopes of achieving a better reading of the text.

The divisions in biblical studies have meant that Black scholars have often felt torn between traditions of biblical interpretation that center cultural questions to the exclusion of what the text might say or force the cultural questions to the side for the sake of respectability. That is a false choice. We can have both. Depending on the context we can place more emphasis on the text or the questions that our culture proposes.

This dialogical method opens up Black biblical interpretation to other interpretive traditions. If our cultures and histories define the totality of our interpretive enterprise, the price of admission can be complete acquiescence to that culture's particularities. This is as true with European domination of the text as it would be if Black culture completely sets the contours for the debate. But if we all read the biblical text assuming that God is able to speak a coherent word to us through it, then we can discuss the meanings our varied cultures have gleaned from the Scriptures. What I have in mind then is a unified mission in which our varied cultures turn to the text in dialogue with one another to discern the mind of Christ. That means in the providence of God, I need Ugandan biblical interpretation, because the experiences of Ugandans mean they are able to bring their unique insights to the conversation. African American exegesis, then, precisely because it is informed by the Black experience, has the potential to be universal when added to the chorus of believers through time and across cultures.

Throughout the rest of this book my goal is to demonstrate and embody the Black ecclesial interpretive model. In chapter two, I sketch out a New Testament theology of policing because a pressing question for the Black Christian today is the relationship between the populace and those entrusted with the task of serving and protecting our communities. In chapter three, I ask what the New Testament has to say about political protest and the witness of the church. I show that the Scriptures provide Black Christians with a bevy of examples and resources that inform the church's witness to the watching world. Chapter four addresses the question of justice. I argue that the New Testament (drawing mostly on the gospel of Luke) paints a picture of the just society that is distinctly Christian and speaks directly to the hopes of Black Christians. Chapter five tackles the question of ethnicity. Here my concern is quite simple. I want to find out whether God saves me from my blackness (the colorblind kingdom model) or whether my blackness is a unique manifestation of the glory of God. Chapter six addresses the question of Black anger and pain. Given our historic mistreatment, is there a way to deal with our frustrations and anger in a way that heals us? The final chapter addresses the question behind most of our questions, namely the relationship between the Bible and slavery. In the end, we come to the freedom of the enslaved person. I have also included a brief appendix (bonus track) that chronicles a little more of my examination of early Black Christianity that had to be omitted from this chapter because of concerns for space. Those interested in this conversation are encouraged to read the "bonus track" first before going on to the rest of the book.

Most of these topics could function as books in their own right. Space will preclude a discussion of these matters in full. Scholars might complain that I didn't say more or dialogue with more positions. That was not my goal. When the choice was between detailed analysis and readability my instincts were often the latter. Rather than address all the issues in every text, my goal instead is to point toward a way of Bible reading that reflects the tradition that formed me and continues to form a generation of scholars and clergy. This work is written to honor their too-often-ignored witness.

This book then is not an apologetic attempting to explain away all the problematic parts of church history nor is it a defense of the entire Black Christian tradition. Instead it is an attempt to show that the instincts and habits of *Black biblical interpretation* can help us use the Bible to address the issues of the day. It is an attempt to show that for Black Christians the very process of interpreting the Bible can function as an exercise in hope and connect us to the faith of our ancestors. More than that, it is one attempt of one son to do justice to the faith given to him by his mother, as a representative of a tradition that has borne Black people in this country up under suffering for centuries. It is an assertion of a claim, namely that the Black ecclesial tradition has something to say that strikes a different note than the standard options often given to students of the Bible and theology. It is a love letter from a somewhat wayward son of the Black church who did not appreciate its depth and power until he went searching for the truth—and found that it was at home all along.

TWO

FREEDOM IS NO FEAR

THE NEW TESTAMENT AND A
THEOLOGY OF POLICING

■ ■ ■

I'll tell you what freedom is. Freedom is no fear.

NINA SIMONE

Shall not the Judge of all the earth do what is just?

GENESIS 18:25

BY THE TIME I WAS SIXTEEN, I had no doubt that football would be
my path to college.[1] The letters and phone calls from college coaches
had just begun, but my school had a rich tradition of sending its
better athletes to university. All I had to do was perform on the field
and stay out of trouble. At this point in high school, I had developed
a sufficient buffer between myself and the violence of my neighborhood. I knew how to navigate the parties and neighborhoods of
Northwest Huntsville. People knew me, not as a criminal, but as
someone it wasn't wise to bother. My grades were good enough to

---

[1] I was wrong; such is the exuberance of youth.

make getting into college a foregone conclusion.[2] Therefore, when I speak of trouble I did not have in mind my own behavior.

I was afraid of running into problems with the police—that I might find myself in an encounter that spun out of control. Why did I have this fear? I grew up in the aftermath of the Rodney King incident, which, in the era before cell phone videos, was an unheard of piece of evidence that confirmed Black fears.

Rodney King had led the police on a high speed chase through Los Angeles. Eventually the police got him to stop, and after he exited the car, he was savagely beaten by four officers. The entire country saw that video and the pictures of King's bruised body. But King's beating did not create the fear. Most of us had our own stories, which might not have been as dramatic, but which still left lasting impressions. Driving while Black was not a problem that we imagined.[3]

By my junior year, then, I was wary. To prevent any problems, I developed a ritual whenever I went out with my friends. I volunteered to drive because I did not smoke or drink. Before getting into my car, I made sure that none of us had anything illegal. No drugs, alcohol, or weapons entered my vehicle. As much as it depended on me, I had accounted for everything. We all traveled clean, and I drove. This seemed like a safe path through my last years of high school and into university.

One night we had plans to go to the mall and later a party in the same part of town. As you can imagine, the main road leading to the mall was well travelled by many a teen on a Friday night. We decided to stop at a gas station on that road and fill up before continuing on

---

[2]I was not a stellar student, but stellar wasn't required of football players.
[3]The best short article can be found here: Christopher Ingraham, "You Really Can Get Pulled Over for Driving While Black, Federal Statistics Show," *Washington Post*, September 9, 2014, www.washingtonpost.com/news/wonk/wp/2014/09/09/you-really-can-get -pulled-over-for-driving-while-black-federal-statistics-show.

with the night's festivities. While at the station, we saw some of our friends who were heading in the same direction. We told them about the party and encouraged them to meet us there. After I finished filling up the tank, I got ready to leave. Then I noticed that a Black SUV had pulled up quite close to my car. I thought that was odd. He would get his gas soon enough. Then another SUV drove up to my left and another parked in front of my car. I thought I was being car jacked, but who would car jack someone less than a mile from the mall at a well-lit gas station? The mystery was solved when the officers came filing out of the SUV. They told us to put our hands where they could see them. I remember my friend saying that he wasn't putting his hands anywhere. Right then my future flashed before my eyes. Had all my planning been for naught? Would my dreams unravel at the local Stop & Shop in exchange for a bag of chips and a few gallons of fuel?

I told my friend to be quiet and do as the officer said. We complied. Then they told us to get out of the car. We complied. I asked the officer what was going on. Why had we been detained? He said that this gas station was a known drug spot and that he had seen us conducting a drug deal. I couldn't help but think that was also a well-known place to acquire gas. But what could we do? He asked for all our licenses. Those that had them gave them up without protest. The officers then proceeded to check us and the car for anything illegal. I felt powerless and angry. The whole thing lasted less than twenty minutes. They found nothing. I expected some apology for what had just happened to us, some further explanation of what we had done other than being young and Black and at a gas station. Instead, they gave us back our licenses and told us we were free to go.

After it was over, I no longer had any desire to go to the mall. Instead, I took everyone home and called it a night. The next morning,

I couldn't help but reflect on how close I came to losing it all: the football scholarship, the path out of poverty, the chance to help my family. I had been briefly terrorized. I wish that I could say that this was the only or the most egregious thing that happened to me. By my count, I have been stopped somewhere between seven and ten times on the road or for existing in public spaces for no crime other than being Black.

These words may make it seem as if I dislike police officers. I do not. I have known many good police officers. I recognize the dangers that they face and the difficulties inherent in the vocation they choose. But a difficult job does not absolve one of criticism; it puts the criticism in a wider framework. That wider framework must also include, if we are going to be complete, the history of the police's interaction with people of color in this country. If the difficulty of the job provides context, so does the historic legal enforcement of racial discrimination and the terror visited on Black bodies. We must tell the whole story, as difficult as that telling might be.

Therefore, the question of how the police treats its citizens is a pressing issue in the lives of Black people. Surprisingly, despite the ongoing concerns of African Americans, this subject has seen very little reflection in the standard works on New Testament ethics.[4] Is the guild correct? Is the issue of the state's treatment of its citizens a subject foreign to the New Testament such that Black folk looking to these texts will find little succor?

The New Testament provides the beginning of a Christian theology of policing in two places, which we will consider in turn. First, I will examine the much maligned and misunderstood Romans

---

[4]See, for example, the otherwise excellent works of Richard A. Burridge, *Imitating Jesus: An Inclusive Approach to New Testament Ethics* (Grand Rapids, MI: Eerdmans, 2007) and Richard Hays, *The Moral Vision of the New Testament: A Contemporary Introduction to New Testament Ethics* (San Francisco: HarperSanFrancisco, 1996).

13:1-7. I will argue that scholars neglect the overlapping role of soldier and police officer in ancient Rome.[5] This neglect has led them to ignore the fact that Paul's words on the sword, and their link to the will and limits of the state, bear directly on the question of how the state polices its residents. Therefore, Romans 13:1-7 is a foundational passage for constructing a New Testament theology of policing. After establishing its importance, I will argue that Romans 13:1-7 has a lot more going on than advocating for a passive populace that pays its taxes and defers to those in power. I will maintain that Romans 13:1-7 asserts the sovereignty of God over the state. Paul says that the state's policing duties should never be a terror to those who are innocent. Building upon the insights on the link between the soldier and the police officer, we will turn our attention to the ministry of John the Baptist as it's recorded in Luke's Gospel. There we will see him calling on the soldiers/law enforcement officers to do their job with integrity. I will close with a brief analysis of the implications of our exegesis for Christian engagement with the question of policing.

THE ISSUE IS BIGGER THAN YOU THINK:
ROMANS 13:1-2 AND THE PROBLEM OF EVIL RULERS

Romans 13:1-2 does not, on first glance, seem to be a productive place to begin to speak about the *limits* that God places on the treatment of its citizens. It reads:

> Let every person be subject to the governing authorities; for there is no authority except from God, and those authorities that exist have been instituted by God. Therefore whoever resists authority resists what God has appointed, and those who resist will incur judgment. (Rom 13:1-2)

---

[5]Christopher J. Fuhrmann, *Policing the Roman Empire: Soldiers, Administration, and Public Order* (Oxford, UK: Oxford University Press, 2012).

The focus of this passage appears to be individuals, not the state. Furthermore, Paul tells those individuals to submit to those in authority because they have been placed there by *God*. Those who resist these authorities run the risk, then, of opposing God's will. Paul's lack of qualification here has been a cause of concern for many.[6]

Do we not have a case in which the proper Christian response to mistreatment is not revolution, but obedience under suffering in the hopes of an eschatological righting of wrongs? Christian eschatology is a much-maligned area of reflection. The hope of new creation is often portrayed as an opiate lulling us into complacency. Eschatology, however, need not be dismissed as some small thing. The coming kingdom remains a central pillar of theology that not only gives us hope for the future, but also negates the power of those who can kill the body but do no more (Mt 10:28). Nonetheless, I think that Paul has more in mind here than some flattened sub-biblical form of meekness.

We need to recognize that critics of Paul and Romans 13:1-2 have not gone far enough. The problem is not that, according to their interpretation, Paul forbids rebelling against wicked rulers. The problem is the *wicked rulers* themselves. The issue, I want to suggest, is not merely exegetical; it is also philosophical. The path forward is not only found in a new exegetical insight, a new twist on a verb here or a noun there.[7] The way beyond the impasse is to pursue the logic of the text to the end.

---

[6]Leander E. Keck, in *Romans*, Abingdon New Testament Commentaries (Nashville: Abingdon Press, 2005), says, "It is not the opaqueness of this passage that has distressed and divided interpreters but its clarity" (311); See also R. Cassidy, "The Politicization of Paul: Romans 13:1-7 in Recent Discussion," *The Expository Times* 121, no 8 (2010): 383-89.
[7]This should not imply that the contextual framework within which we place the text does not matter. There are some significant examples of readings of Romans that take our own contexts and the wider letter seriously. For one attempt at such a reading see Monya A. Stubbs, "Subjection, Reflection, Resistance: An African American Reading of the Three-Dimensional Process of Empowerment in Romans 13 and the Free-Market," in *Navigating Romans through Cultures: Challenging Readings by Charting a New Course* (New York: T&T Clark, 2004), 171-98.

Therefore we must ask why a good God, who is sovereign over all, would allow evil rulers to come to power? Stated differently, the question is not about our submission to wicked rulers, but their very existence. The criticism of Paul, then, is theodicy in a different form. Asking what we are to do when those tasked with governing us use that power to do harm is simply another way of asking why there is harm at all.

One response to the problem of evil has been to posit the cross and resurrection as God's answer to the question. We do not worship a God who sits apart, but who enters human pain and redeems it from within. The Christian is not given a series of deductive proofs that solve the problem of evil to our satisfaction. We are given an act of love that woos us. And we know that this wooing isn't a false promise because the resurrection proves that God is sovereign over life and death. Our focus on eschatology in any case is not unique. The nihilist is just as driven by their eschatology. It's just that his or hers is devoid of hope: let us eat and drink for tomorrow we die.

But we have drifted from Paul. Does the apostle have anything to say about how the state treats its citizens and our public response to that treatment that goes beyond submission? Yes. I suggest that Paul's words about submission to governing authorities must be read in light of four realities: (1) Paul's use of Pharaoh *in Romans* as an example of God removing authorities through human agents shows that his prohibition against resistance is not absolute; (2) the wider Old Testament testifies to God's use of human agents to take down corrupt governments; (3) in light of the first two propositions, we can affirm that God is active through human beings even when we can't discern the exact role we play; (4) therefore, Paul's words should be seen as more of a limit on our discernment than on God's activities.

First, Paul and Pharaoh. Romans 9:17 reads, "For scripture says to Pharaoh: 'I have raised you up for this very purpose of showing my power in you, so that my name may be proclaimed in all the earth.'" God, according to the apostle, is glorified through his judgment of wicked kings.

God removed Pharaoh because of his unjust and tyrannical rule. Exodus makes it clear that it is because of the economic exploitation, enslavement, and harsh treatment of Israel:

> Then the Lord said, "I have observed the misery of my people who are in Egypt; *I have heard their cry on account of their taskmasters. Indeed, I know their sufferings,* and I have come down to deliver them from the Egyptians, and to bring them up out of that land to a good and broad land, a land flowing with milk and honey, to the country of the Canaanites, the Hittites, the Amorites, the Perizzites, the Hivites, and the Jebusites. *The cry of the Israelites has now come to me; I have also seen how the Egyptians oppress them.* So come, I will send you to Pharaoh to bring my people, the Israelites, out of Egypt." (Ex 3:7-10, emphasis added)

Pharaoh's destruction, as it was presented in the book of Exodus, is largely the work of God. But God acts through *Moses*. Paul alludes to this story to speak about God's sovereignty in Romans. Therefore, Paul knew and discussed in Romans an example of someone who *did not* merely submit to their authorities, namely Moses. This means that in Romans 13:1-2, Paul either has some qualification in mind or he considered Moses sinful.[8] Furthermore, we have numerous examples of Old Testament passages where God uses human beings to bring down governments for their wickedness.[9] Based on

---

[8]Surprisingly, Paul's use of the Pharaoh narrative is almost universally ignored in considerations of Romans 13. The notable exception being Beverly Roberts Gaventa, "Reading Romans 13 with Simone Weil: Toward a More Generous Hermeneutic," *Journal of Biblical Literature* 136 (2017): 3-22.

[9]Daniel 7:1-28, for example, lays out a whole unfolding history of nations rising and falling according to the will of Israel's sovereign Lord.

these two realities, I believe that Paul does not simply delay the righting of wrongs until the eschaton. Instead, Paul shows rightful skepticism about our ability to discern how we are functioning in God's wider purposes. Stated differently, God brings his judgment against corrupt institutions through *humans* in his own time, and we are not given insight into our proper role in such matters.[10]

Moses might point the way forward. In his younger days he sees the oppression of his fellow Israelites and responds by killing an Egyptian (Ex 2:11-15). We know that Moses had properly diagnosed the problem of Israel's slavery, but his solution was ill conceived. Later, God in his own time does bring lasting liberation to his people and links it to proper worship and the transformation of the nation (Ex 3:1-22).

I maintain, then, that we read Romans 13:1-2 as a statement about the sovereignty of God *and* the limits of human discernment. We are allowed to discern and even condemn evil like the prophets did. We are allowed to resist like the Hebrew midwives, Daniel, Shadrach, Meshach, and Abednego. Nonetheless, we cannot claim divine sanction for the proper timing and method of solving the problems we discern.[11] Again, this does not place limits on our ability as Christians to call evil by its name, but it does obligate us to be willing to suffer the consequences of living in a fallen world. We recognize that the state has been given its responsibilities. We are not anarchists, but we do recognize that the state is in fact *under God*. The state has duties, and we can hold them accountable even if it means that we

---

[10]Stubbs suggests that Paul might be a little more pragmatic than I give him credit for. She says, "If this passage is read in the light of its surrounding verses (12:1–13:14), it reads less like a prescriptive demand and more like a call for Roman Christians to acknowledge their social reality in relation to the Roman state which is part of the existence of life in the Christian community." Stubbs, "Subjection, Reflection, Resistance," 172.

[11]I contend that Paul's theology of government is not much different from what we encounter in Daniel 2:20-21, which says the following: "Blessed be the name of God from age to age, / for wisdom and power are his. / He changes times and seasons, / deposes kings and sets up kings."

suffer for doing so peacefully. This suffering is only futile if the resurrection is a lie. If the resurrection is true, and the Christian stakes his or her entire existence on its truthfulness, then our peaceful witness testifies to a new and better way of being human that transcends the endless cycle of violence. Paul, then, in Romans 13:1-2 is not far from Jesus who tells his disciples that those who live by the sword die by it (Mt 26:52).

POLICING THE EMPIRE

Although Paul's words to individuals have received the bulk of attention for exegetes, it is his words concerning the state that point the way to a Christian theology of policing. Paul grounds his call for submission to the state with a description of what the state should do:

> For rulers are not a terror to good conduct, but to bad. Do you wish to have no fear of the authority? Then do what is good, and you will receive its approval; for it is God's servant for your good. But if you do what is wrong, you should be afraid, for the authority does not bear the sword in vain! (Rom 13:3-4)

Two exegetical insights and one historical note will be crucial to our interpretation of this passage. First, the historical. Many have noted that "bear the sword" has connections to the Roman military. The sword refers to the actions of the military at the behest of those in authority.[12] However, Fuhrmann has argued persuasively that the rise of the Empire carried with it an increase in the "policing" activities of soldiers.[13] Therefore, I contend that Paul's words here can be seen as a comment on the role that police officers should play in the body politic. To this historical note we add two exegetical insights that

---

[12]Robert Jewett, *Romans: A Commentary*, Hermeneia (Minneapolis, MN: Fortress, 2007), 796; Leon Morris, *The Epistle to the Romans*, PNTC (Grand Rapids, MI: Eerdmans, 1987), 463-64.
[13]Fuhrmann, *Policing the Roman Empire*.

should not be too controversial. First, in Romans 13:3-4, it is the state's attitude, not the soldier/officer as a vocation that stands at the center of Paul's concerns. Stated differently, Paul recognizes that the state has a tremendous influence on how the soldier/officer treats its citizens. Thus, if there is to be a reform it must be structural and not merely individualistic. This is grounds in a democracy for a structural advocacy on behalf of the powerless. Second, Paul says that the government should not be a source of fear for the innocent. This problem of innocent fearfulness continues to plague encounters between Black persons and law enforcement. Again Paul's words provide guidance on the shape reform must take.

THE ROMAN CHRISTIAN AND THE SOLDIER/OFFICER

In order to understand Paul's words about the "sword," we need to do a few things. First, we must define what we mean by police. Then we need to show that in Paul's time soldiers performed a policing role by outlining the ways in which they policed the empire. This will lead to some practical thoughts on how Roman Christians might have encountered the sword.

In referring to Roman soldiers as police, I do not mean that they functioned like modern police whose sole job is to investigate crimes, make arrests, and testify in court.[14] When I refer to police officers, I have in mind, "any organized unit of men under official command whose duties involved maintaining public order and state control in a civilian setting."[15] Did Roman soldiers perform this policing role? Yes.

In 48 BC Octavian defeated Mark Antony and Cleopatra. This made him the sole power throughout the Roman world. One of the first things he did was transform the Roman militia into a standing

---

[14]Furhmann, *Policing the Roman Empire*, 4.
[15]Furhmann, *Policing the Roman Empire*, 6.

army. This standing army was responsible for maintaining public order.[16] Part of this maintenance of public order included, "guard duty, calming public disturbance," and "crime investigation."[17] In Rome itself, Octavian created the Praetorian guard whose responsibility included the policing duties mentioned above and seeing to the safety of Octavian and his family.[18] The best estimates maintain that there were nine cohorts of the guard with between five hundred and one thousand soldiers in each cohort. These soldier/police officers were separated from their legions outside the city and lived in and among the people.[19] They did not wear military uniforms and were often paid better than normal soldiers.[20] Alongside his guard, Octavian set up the *vigiles*, a group whose initial mandate was to prevent arson and put out fires. Their role expanded, however, to include investigating petty crimes.[21] When combined, the *vigiles* and the Praetorian guard were about ten thousand people charged with maintaining order in the city. This is roughly one officer per one hundred people.[22] Therefore, Paul's words about the sword would not have been an abstraction. Roman Christians would have come into contact, knowingly or not, with the policing power of the state on a regularly basis.

We have established that the closest thing to a police force in Rome would be the soldiers who had been stationed in the city for the express purpose of maintaining order. We have also shown that they would not be a peripheral part of a Roman Christian's life, but that a Roman Christian could expect to interact with the officers/soldiers

---

[16]Pat Southern, *The Roman Army: A Social and Institutional History* (Santa Barbara, CA: ABC-CLIO, 2006), 96-97.

[17]Furhmann, *Policing the Roman Empire*, 7.

[18]Southern, *Roman Army*, 115.

[19]Southern, *Roman Army*, 8.

[20]Southern, *Roman Army*, 115.

[21]Furhmann, *Policing the Roman Empire*, 117.

[22]Furhmann notes that this is more than the city of New York, which has one officer per 190 people. Furhmann, *Policing the Roman Empire*, 118.

quite regularly. We have evidence of this regularity in the New Testament itself, which periodically depicts interactions with soldiers.

Can we say more? Where exactly might a Christian encounter this police force? Understanding how the Christian might encounter this police force is crucial if we want to understand the actual interactions between Christians and the "sword."

Augustus justified his rule by lauding the "peace" that he brought to the empire. In his famous *Res Gestae*, he relies on an ancient legend about the closing of the gate of Janus Quirinus to demonstrate the unprecedented peace he brought to Rome. He said, "Our ancestors wanted Janus Quirinus to be closed when throughout all the rule of the Roman people, by land and sea, peace had been secured through victory. Although before my birth it had been closed twice in all in recorded memory from the founding of the city, the senate voted three times in my principate that it be closed."[23] This peace was not merely the result of defeating enemies abroad; it was also about safety at home. Part of this safety entailed the curtailing of crime in the city. This involved setting up cohorts in troubled parts of the city and investigating crimes. These soldiers also worked alongside the *vigiles*, who functioned as something close to a night watch. They also oversaw gladiator events and other major festivals in the city's life.[24] Another neglected aspect of the soldier's role was assisting in tax collection. Tax collectors in Rome were known for their corruption, often over, charging the people and demanding bribes.[25] The soldiers in imperial Rome often functioned as the muscle behind the threats of these tax collectors.[26]

---

[23]Augustus, *Res Gestae*, trans. Thomas Bushnell (n.p.: n.p., 1998), 13, http://classics.mit .edu/Augustus/deeds.html.

[24]Furhmann, *Policing the Roman Empire*, 117, 129.

[25]Pheme Perkins, "Taxes in the New Testament," *The Journal of Religious Ethics* 12 (1984): 182-200.

[26]Perkins, "Taxes in the New Testament," 183.

There is one more group that we must mention to round out our discussion of the policing in Rome: the *Aediles* and their staff. In the days of the republic, their job was to care for the temples and some of the public works of the city. Eventually, this role expanded to include maintaining public order. They also oversaw the markets by making sure that taxes were paid and the scales at the market were just. The oversight of the scales also led merchants to bribe *Aediles* and their staff so that the merchants could cheat their customers.[27]

A Roman Christian, then, might encounter the police if they found themselves in the wrong part of town late at night. Given that we know the early Roman Christians were not on the whole rich, living in the wrong part of town would have been the daily experience of many.[28] Moreover, they might be questioned by the *vigiles* or Octavian's guard simply for living in this neighborhood. They might have been bullied by officers trying to get a few extra dollars when tax collection season came around. Christian shop owners might have been pressured to pay the "fee" for doing business or risk being beat out by a competitor. Whenever the city was alive with festival and celebration, the Roman Christian might have had to watch out for an anxious officer who was keen to keep said festivities from spiraling out of control. In short, at any moment in the lives of Roman church members, they might come face to face with the state and its sword. Stated differently, the Roman Christian's interaction with the power of the state bears some striking similarities to the potential encounters African Americans might have with the police in our day.

---

[27]Furhmann, *Policing the Roman Empire*, 60-61.
[28]See Peter Lampe's *From Paul to Valentinus: Christians at Rome in the First Two Centuries* (Minneapolis, MN: Fortress Press, 2003).

PAUL, STRUCTURAL REFORM, AND THE ABSENCE OF FEAR

Having sketched the realities of policing in ancient Rome we can turn to exegesis proper. In Romans 13:3-4 Paul focuses on the authorities, not the officers themselves. He says, "Rulers are not a terror to good conduct, but to bad. Do you wish to have no fear of the authority? Then do what is good, and you will receive its approval." Here Paul recognizes that the soldier's attitude toward the people who reside in the city will in large part be determined by those who give the orders.[29] The problem, if there is one, does not reside solely in those who bear the sword, but those who direct it. In other words, Paul does not focus on individual actions, but on power structures.

For the American Christian this means that he or she has to face the fact that our government has crafted laws over the course of centuries, not decades, that were designed to disenfranchise Black people.[30] These laws were then enforced by means of the state's power of the sword. Historically in America, the issue has been institutional corporate sin undergirded by the policing power of the state.

What does Paul's focus on *structure* mean for a Christian theology of policing? It means that the same government that created the structures has some responsibility to see those wrongs righted and injustices undone. Furthermore, if the power truly resides *with the people* in a democratic republic, then the Christian's first responsibility is to make sure that those who direct the sword in our culture direct that sword in ways in keeping with our values. We can and must hold elected officials responsible for the collective actions of the agents of the state who act on our behalf. Furthermore,

---

[29]I use the language of "reside in the city" purposefully. Most were not citizens of Rome.
[30]Thomas Hoyt Jr., "Interpreting Biblical Scholarship for the Black Church Tradition," in *The Stony Road We Trod: African American Biblical Interpretation*, ed. Cain Hope Felder (Minneapolis, MN: Fortress Press, 1991), 17-39.

as participants in a free society, we have the ability to shape public opinion about what crime is and how criminals should be viewed. We can create a society where those who are suspected of breaking the law are treated as image bearers worthy of respect. A Christian theology of policing, then, must grow out of a Christian theology of persons. This Christian theology of policing must remember that the state is *only* a steward or caretaker of persons. It did not *create* them and it does not own or define them. God is our creator, and he will have a word for those who attempt to mar the image of God in any person. We are being the Christians God called us to be when we remind the state of the limits of its power.

A second series of exegetical insights follow from the first. Paul says that the rulers (who control the police) are not a terror to those engaged in good conduct. Paul states this as a fact. However, given what we said above about God's ability to judge nations and rulers for corrupt practices, we can see that Paul speaks of an ideal. He knows that some rulers are a terror to those who are good. Paul mentioned a ruler (Pharaoh) earlier in Romans that was a terror, and that ruler experienced God's judgment. In Romans 13:1-7, then, Paul outlines rulers' responsibilities as God's servants without directly addressing the problem of *evil* rulers. I contend that in absence of that explanation of Romans 13:1-7, we are free to use Paul's reference to Egypt and the wider biblical account to fill in the gap.

Now we come to the heart of it. Black hope for policing is not that complicated. Paul articulates that hope quite plainly in Romans 13:4. We want to live free of fear. When I am pulled over for a traffic stop, I am afraid precisely because the police have been a source of terror in my own life and the lives of my people. This terror trickled down from a national government that often viewed our skin as dangerous. As I entered the last years of high school, I was not afraid of doing anything wrong that might cost me a trip to college. If that happened it would be on me. I could deal with that. But I was afraid of being perceived as a threat because I could not in a few tense moments of interaction with law enforcement argue or wish away centuries of mistrust. I am afraid still because I worry that my sons or daughters might experience the same terror that marked the life of their father and my ancestors before me.

This fear might seem unwarranted to some. I am tempted to list statistics about Black folks and our treatment at the hands of the police. But I am skeptical that statistics will convince those hostile to our cause. Furthermore, statistics are unnecessary for those who carry the experience of being Black in this country in their hearts. We know, and this book is for us.

Paul provides a few starting points on how Christians can think about policing from a biblical/theological perspective. He rightly focuses on those who control the sword and not merely the individual. This gives the Christian thinker and advocate the space to think structurally about how a just society should treat its people. Paul also speaks about the absence of fear, a central concern for Black folks. Yes, Paul does speak about the Christian's responsibility to the government. This is fine. We do not want anarchy. We gladly acknowledge the potential goods of government. We also recognize the church's ability to discern evil in government actions even if we lack the sovereignty over history to know when God will bring judgment. Nonetheless, we must always remember that Paul's words on submission to government come in the context of a Bible that shows God active in history to bring about his purposes. God lifts up and God tears down. To avoid that tearing down, those who have the task of government must do all in their power to construct a society in which Black persons can live and move and work freely.

THE WITNESS OF JOHN THE BAPTIST AND
THE RESPONSIBILITIES OF POLICE OFFICERS

If our thesis that the soldier is the closest thing to a modern police officer is true, then encounters with soldiers in the New Testament can provide us with important insights into a Christian theology of policing. John the Baptist's ministry in the Gospel of Luke provides us with just such an occurrence.[31]

It is important to remember how John functions in the wider Christian narrative. [32] According to the Gospel writers, God appointed John as a herald of the coming Messiah and of the messianic age.[33] All of them associate him with the figure described in Isaiah. Here we will focus on Luke's version:

> As it is written in the book of the words of the prophet Isaiah,
> "The voice of one crying out in the wilderness:
> 'Prepare the way of the Lord,
>   make his paths straight.
> Every valley shall be filled,
>   and every mountain and hill shall be made low,
> and the crooked shall be made straight,
>   and the rough ways made smooth;
> and all flesh shall see the salvation of God.'" (Lk 3:4-6)

In the Isaiah quote, the prophet does not prepare the way for the coming messiah; the voice in the wilderness prepares us for the advent of God. This raises the question of the identity of this coming king. In any case, John the Baptist's call to repentance is a command

---

[31]On the importance of John the Baptist in Luke's Gospel, see Clint Burnett, "Eschatological Prophet of Restoration: Luke's Theological Portrait of John the Baptist in Luke 3:1-6," *Neotestamentica* 47 (2013): 1-24.

[32]The definitive academic study on John the Baptist is probably *John the Baptist in History and Theology* (Studies on Personalities of the New Testament) by Joel Marcus.

[33]See Luke 1:68-79.

to prepare for God's coming. To refuse to change, in John's estimation, entails missing out on the new exodus to a new inheritance that Jesus will accomplish.

Those who heed John's call to preparation have one question: What must we do to participate in the coming kingdom? John responds with practical suggestions to different groups. The one that is important for our purposes is his response to the soldiers/police officers. He tells them, "Do not extort money from anyone by threats or false accusation, and be satisfied with your wages" (Lk 3:14). If Romans 13:3-4 focuses on the responsibility of the state, then Luke 3:14 gives us a picture of the individual law enforcement officer's responsibilities. In what follows I examine the implications of what John says by focusing on issues of (1) policing and power, (2) policing and the image of God (again), and (3) policing and money.

First we must address the question of the identity of these soldiers. Are they Jews or Gentiles? What is the exact nature of their work? Given the mention of the tax collectors in the previous verses and John's discussion of extortion, he probably has in mind those soldiers who assisted in tax collection.[34] Yet his advice would hold true regardless of the exact nature of their work. Given their ability to use violence, it is incumbent on police agents to do their work with integrity.

John begins by condemning extortion. Do not underestimate the weight of this critique. Extortion goes beyond mere bribes. Extortion involves using your *power* to prey on the weak. Extortion is only possible when the exhorted have no recourse. This means that John

---

[34]John Nolland, *Luke 1–9:20*, WBC 35A (Grand Rapids, MI: Zondervan, 1989), 150; Bovon says that "these soldiers could be mercenaries of Herod Antipas, who ruled not only Galilee but also Perea." François Bovon, *Luke 1: A Commentary on the Gospel of Luke 1:1–9:50*, Hermeneia 63a (Minneapolis, MN: Fortress Press, 2002), 397; Culpepper says that they "were probably not Romans but local mercenaries serving the Herods or the Roman procurator. Their role, therefore, was similar to that of the toll collectors." R. Alan Culpepper, "The Gospel of Luke," in *The Gospel of Luke–The Gospel of John*, NIB 9 (Nashville: Abingdon Press, 1995), 85.

was concerned with a form of policing in which those who have power use it as a means of pursuing their own agenda at the cost of those most at risk. For this reason, his criticism of false accusations should not be separated from extortion because false accusations often undergird extortion. If the people being extorted refused to comply they might find themselves "accused" of crimes that they did not commit.

John also might have in mind a soldier offering up a person for a crime to satisfy the whim of their superior or to achieve some political end. This giving over of bodies as sacrificial offerings for the maintenance of the status quo denies the *imago Dei* in each of us. The story of Jesus' crucifixion contains the paradigmatic false accusation. When John's Gospel recounts Pilate's unintentionally profound words, "Behold the man," it speaks to Jesus as the one true human who came to restore us all. At the same time, John makes it clear that even as an innocent person condemned to die Jesus is in fact a *person*. This is the Black claim on the conscience of those who police us. See us as persons worthy of respect in every instance. Jesus' treatment by the soldiers strikes us as egregious because he was innocent of the charges (Mt 27:27-30), but do the guilty deserve beatings and mockery? Matthew 27:27-30 speaks to how a corrupt system can distort the souls of those charged with functioning in a broken system. John calls on those in that system to rise above the temptation to dehumanize and act with integrity.

Finally, John calls on those who police to be satisfied with their wages. This again points to the link between policing and money. Soldiers/officers must be satisfied with what they receive for the work that they do. In our day, this speaks to excessive fines and tickets given to the poor that only serve to enrich the state. For John the Baptist, money can never trump justice. What does John add to a Christian theology of policing? He adds the personal responsibility and integrity of the officers themselves. He calls upon those with power to use that power to uphold the inherent dignity of all residents and to never use that power for their own ends.

CONCLUSION

We have only scratched the surface of the New Testament's portrayal of policing, but I take it that my larger point has been made. The closest parallel to the modern police were the soldiers tasked with the work of keeping order in the cities and towns of the empire. These soldiers, especially in Rome, touched on every aspect of the Christian life. Although Paul focuses on the responsibilities that individuals have to the state, in the course of his discussion he lays out the responsibilities that the state has to individuals. The state must remember that it is not divine or infallible. It is a steward of that which belongs to God. Romans 9:17 demonstrates that said stewardship can be removed. Nonetheless, that stewardship involves police work. Therefore, those who rule countries are responsible for the culture of policing that they encourage. As Christians, it is part of our calling to remind those charged with governing of their need to create an atmosphere in which people are able to live without fear. This has been the Black person's repeated lament. We should not live in fear. Good should be rewarded and evil punished. The United States, historically and in the present, has not done that. Instead it has used the sword to instill a fear that has been passed down from generation to generation in Black homes and churches— but that fear has never had the final word. Instead Black Christians remembered that we need not fear those who can only kill the body. At our best and most Christian moments, we have demanded our birthrights as children of God. But that right should not be purchased at the price of our blood or mental health. A Christian theology of policing, then, is a theology of freedom.

If Paul spoke to the power of the state and the sword, the Baptist turned his eye toward the individual soldier. He called them, not to heroic feats of physical bravery, but to heroic virtue. He reminded them that their power need not turn them into villains who exploit. They could become champions for the weak. A Christian theology of policing, then, looks to the state and calls it to remember its duties. It looks to the officer and demands that said officer recognize the tremendous responsibility and potential of the work that they do. If we undertake this task of calling on the officer and the state to be what God called them to be, then maybe the hopes of Black folks as they relate to the police in this country might be fulfilled.

THREE

TIRED FEET, RESTED SOULS

THE NEW TESTAMENT AND THE POLITICAL WITNESS OF THE CHURCH

■ ■ ■

My feets is tired, but my soul is rested.

MOTHER POLLARD

Have I now become your enemy by telling you the truth?

GALATIANS 4:16

ON APRIL 12, 1963, EIGHT CLERGY—two Methodist bishops, two Episcopal bishops, one Roman Catholic Bishop, a Rabbi, a Presbyterian, and a Baptist—wrote a letter addressed to the citizens of Alabama. This was their second such proclamation. Their first, written nearly three months earlier on January 16, was named "An Appeal for Law and Order and Common Sense." It called for an end to violence surrounding civil rights protests in Alabama and implored those on both sides of the divide regarding the civil rights of African Americans to trust the court system. Although it said that "every human being is created in the image of God and is entitled to respect as a fellow human being with all basic rights, privileges, and responsibilities which belong to humanity," it made no strong stand against segregation. It was the epitome of moderation.

Some three months later this group of eight composed another letter. This one contained a not-so-veiled criticism of Martin Luther King Jr. and the Southern Christian Leadership Council (SCLC) whom they characterized as "outsider agitators" whose actions did not further the cause of peace.[1] They questioned the efficacy of the political witness of Rev. Dr. King and others. They pointed out the fact that "such actions as incite to hatred and violence, however technically peaceful those actions may be, have not contributed to the resolution of our local problems. We do not believe that these days of new hope are days when extreme measures are justified in Birmingham."[2] This criticism of King's actions and the Black Christian tradition of protest that undergirded it came from something of a white southern ecumenical consensus. Baptists, Methodists, Presbyterians, Catholics, Episcopalians, and Jewish leaders opposed King.[3]

What we know as the "Letter from a Birmingham Jail" comes as a response not just to eight clergy but to a certain approach to religion (Christianity) that was focused more on law and order than the demands of the gospel. In his reply to these eight clergy, where he explains his reasons for being in Birmingham, King said,

> I am in Birmingham because injustice is here. Just as the prophets of the eighth century B.C. left their villages and carried their "thus saith the Lord" far beyond the boundaries of their home towns, and

---

[1] C. C. J. Carpenter, et al., "A Call for Unity," April 12, 1963, www3.dbu.edu/mitchell/documents/ ACallforUnityTextandBackground.pdf.

[2] Carpenter, et al., "A Call for Unity."

[3] For a review of the eight men and their stories before and after this letter, see S. Jonathan Bass, *Blessed Are the Peacemakers: Martin Luther King, Jr., Eight White Religious Leaders, and the "Letter from Birmingham Jail"* (Baton Rouge, LA: LSU Press, 2001).

just as the Apostle Paul left his village of Tarsus and carried the gospel of Jesus Christ to the far corners of the Greco Roman world, so am I compelled to carry the gospel of freedom beyond my own home town. Like Paul, I must constantly respond to the Macedonian call for aid.[4]

Nearly sixty years after the publication of this letter, the debate around the role of the church in the public square continues. Was King's mission to end segregation and create a just society at all analogous to the work of Paul and the prophets or was it merely partisan politics? Was his public and consistent criticism of the political power structure of his day an element of his pastoral ministry or a distraction from it?

For many Black Christians the answer to this question is self-evident. We have never had the luxury of separating our faith from political action. Due to the era into which it was born, the Black church found it necessary to protest a policy put in place by the state: slavery. When Frederick Douglass asked his famous question, "What to a Slave Is the Fourth of July?," he didn't simply ask a question about the *United States of America*. He asked a question about *American Christianity*. He said:

What, to the American slave, is your 4th of July? I answer; a day that reveals to him, more than all other days in the year, the gross injustice and cruelty to which he is the constant victim. To him, your celebration is a sham; your boasted liberty, an unholy license; your national greatness, swelling vanity; your sounds of rejoicing are empty and heartless; your denunciation of tyrants, brass fronted impudence; your shouts of liberty and equality, hollow mockery; *your prayers and hymns, your sermons and thanksgivings, with all your religious parade and solemnity, are, to Him, mere bombast, fraud, deception, impiety,*

---

[4]Martin Luther King Jr., "Letter from a Birmingham Jail" in *I Have a Dream: Speeches and Writings That Changed the World*, ed. James M. Washington (New York: HarperCollins, 1992), 83-106.

and hypocrisy—a thin veil to cover up crimes which would disgrace a
nation of savages.[5]

By highlighting the hypocrisy of religious celebrations of freedom while enslaving others, Douglass called upon American Christians to live out their faith by establishing a truly equal and free society. He argued that this country could make no claim to any form of greatness until she faced what she has done to Black and Brown bodies.

Does the Bible support Douglass' and Rev. Dr. King's assertions? More pointedly, what does the New Testament have to say about the political witness of the church in response to the oppressive tendencies of the state?

This chapter begins with a criticism and then moves on to the testimonies of Jesus, Paul, and John. My point in this first section is plain enough. I want to show that if our whole political theology is built on faulty readings of 1 Timothy 2:1-4 and Romans 13:1-7, then we are doing a disservice to New Testament evidence of political criticism and protest. After this deconstructive work, I will move on to consider Jesus' discussion of Herod (Lk 13:32), Paul's dismissal of the entire social and political order (Gal 1:4), and John's depiction of Rome (Rev 18). I will close by calling Jesus back to the stage to speak to us about peacemaking (Mt 5:9). We will see that the enslaved and their descendants who took up the work of political action were tapping into an important element of the New Testament witness.

PRAYER, SUBMISSION, AND THE TEXTS WE CENTER

Many popular political theologies of the New Testament begin with Romans 13:1-7 and 1 Timothy 2:1-4. Centering these texts leaves

---

[5]Frederick Douglass, "The Meaning of July Fourth for the Negro," July 5, 1852, http://masshumanities.org/files/programs/douglass/speech_complete.pdf, emphasis added.

Christians with the following duties: (1) submit to the state, (2) pay your taxes, and (3) pray for those in leadership. None of these three duties are in themselves wrong. They are simply limited in scope.

In an American context, the often-unstated belief in our corporate wisdom and goodness undergirds the call to submit to the government and pray. Many believe that given time and space, our government will eventually opt for the good, the just, and the true. Patience (also a Christian virtue) is urged while we fix whatever is broken. We see this belief in our goodness and the call to patience in the letter addressed to Rev. Dr. King that we mentioned above.

African American Christians who suffer and die while we are told to be patient are allowed to wonder what motivates our fellow Christians to begin with these passages. We are also allowed to ask whether 1 Timothy 2:1-4 and Romans 13:1-7, when read together and against Black protest for freedom, are being used to distort the message of the New Testament. As we stated earlier, the question is not the authority of the texts under consideration. Instead we wonder about how they are weaponized in debates about the political witness of the church.

Now is not the time to litigate Romans 13 again.[6] I have already argued that (1) problems that many have with Romans 13:1-2 are more about theodicy than rulers; (2) Romans 9:16 and the wider Old Testament witnesses give us examples of God using *humans* to take down corrupt regimes; and therefore (3) Romans 13:1-7 should be read as a testimony to our inability to discern when God's judgment will arrive. This does not mean that a Christian cannot protest injustice, it means that we cannot claim God's justification for violent revolution. Submission and acquiescence are two different things.

---

[6]See the previous chapter.

But what about 1 Timothy 2:1-4? Doesn't it command us to pray for our rulers? The problem here again is not the call to pray, but its interpretation within a context dedicated to limited Black political expression. 1 Timothy 2:1-4 reads,

> First of all, then, I urge that supplications, prayers, intercessions, and thanksgivings be made for everyone, for kings and all who are in high positions, so that we may lead a quiet and peaceable life in all godliness and dignity. This is right and is acceptable in the sight of God our Savior, who desires everyone to be saved and to come to the knowledge of the truth.

Two things are evident here. Paul's concern is that we pray for all people, not just kings and rulers. The reason we are called to pray is so that we can go about the work of being the people of God without being harassed.[7] Since rulers and kings have much to say about the quality of our lives, we pray that they would give us the space we need to do our work.[8] Black Christians have no problem praying for freedom to pursue the mission of the church unhindered. The question before us is precisely what to do when those in authority stand in the way of us living as free Christians.

The popular misconception that Christians are called to pray and not to speak plainly about contemporary concerns fails to take seriously Paul's own testimony in 1 Timothy about injustice. A quick glance back at chapter one will reveal that Paul makes a not so subtle jab at the practices and laws of Rome.

In 1 Timothy 1:8-11 Paul argues that the law was not put in place for the righteous, but the ungodly. His point is that the law prescribes

---

[7]James D. G. Dunn, "The Letters to Timothy and the Letter to Titus," in *2 Corinthians-Philemon*, NIB 11 (Nashville: Abingdon Press, 2000), 797.

[8]On the link between peace and space to get about the work of salvation, see Clarice J. Martin's "1–2 Timothy, Titus" in *True to Our Native Land: An African American Commentary on the New Testament* (Minneapolis, MN: Fortress Press, 2007), 420.

punishments for wicked, not those obedient to their creator. He then lays out the kinds of ungodliness that the Old Testament law condemns. One of the groups that he singles out are the *andrapodistais*, the slave traders.[9] He groups these slave traders in a category of those who are "contrary to sound doctrine" (1 Tim 1:10). When Paul refers to sound doctrine (*didaskalia*) he has in mind the received teaching of Christians everywhere.

For Paul, then, slave trading is a *theological error* to be shunned by Christians. I am not an expert on Roman slave law, but I am quite sure that there are no laws against slave trading. In fact, slave trading was seen as a good way to make money.[10] Therefore, in the passage immediately preceding Paul's call to pray for leaders he critiques an established practice of the empire as wicked and indicative of ungodly behavior. Prayer for leaders and criticism of their practices are not mutually exclusive ideas. Both have biblical warrant in the same letter.

The purpose of this section has not been to criticize prayer. As an Anglican clergyperson, I pray for our leaders as a part of our weekly Sunday liturgy and my daily private devotions. The goal has been to highlight the problems that occur when this is seen as the totality of our testimony. Now I move on to the more positive examples of public engagement and criticism of rulers in the New Testament beginning with Jesus himself.

---

[9]George W. Knight III, *The Pastoral Epistles*, The New International Greek Testament Commentary (Grand Rapids, MI: Eerdmans, 1992), 86. Harrill argues that Paul doesn't have in mind actual slave traders, but that the writer (not Paul) draws on a Greco-Roman topos in which "slave trader" was used to refer to a generally immoral person, but I think that the connection to the Ten Commandments and the Old Testament prohibitions is stronger. J. A. Harrill, "The Vice of Slave Dealers in Greco-Roman Society: The Use of a Topos in 1 Timothy 1:10," *Journal of Biblical Literature* 118, no. 1 (1999): 97-122. On the link between the vice list in 1 Timothy 1:8-11 and the Decalogue, see the Knight commentary mentioned above.

[10]See A. B. Bosworth, "Vespasian and the Slave Trade," *The Classical Quarterly* 52 (2002): 350-57.

THE TESTIMONY OF JESUS TO POLITICAL RESISTANCE

On one level, we can look at the entirety of Jesus' ministry as an act of political resistance. Luke 1–2 clearly places the birth of Jesus in the context of the reigns of Augustus on one hand and Herod on the other. This placement raises the question of who is the true king of Israel and the world. The Gospels go on to argue that, despite all appearances, the true king with all authority is Jesus (Mt 28:18-20). My focus will not be on Jesus' ministry as a whole. I simply want to explore the implications of his description of Herod during an inter-action with Pharisees.[11]

The scene is brief, but full of meaning. The Pharisees, who throughout Luke's narrative grow more and more suspicious of Jesus' work, warn him to leave the area because Herod seeks his death. Why would Herod perceive Jesus to be a threat? It certainly isn't because Herod is particularly concerned about Jesus transgressing food or Sabbath laws. It is not because Jesus tells people that they should love God and love their neighbors. It is not because Jesus lauds the grace of God and points toward the inclusion of Gentiles. These issues wouldn't be sufficient to rouse Herod from a nap. But something about Jesus causes the Pharisees to tell Jesus to "get away from here, for Herod wants to kill you" (Lk 13:31).

Some accounts of Jesus' life and ministry make his death at the hands of the state unexplainable. Herod did not see Jesus as a danger because he was a compassionate healer who spoke of justice, repentance, and transformation. Herod saw Jesus as a

---

[11]For a brief overview of Herod's relatively uneventful reign, see H. W. Hoehner, "Herod," in *International Standard Bible Encyclopedia (Revised)*, ed. Geoffery W. Bromiley, Accordance electronic edition, version 1.2. (Grand Rapids, MI: Eerdmans, 1979), 694-97; and Morten Hørning Jensen, "Antipas: The Herod Jesus Knew," *Biblical Archaeology Review* 38, no. 5 (2012): 42-46; for a more extensive account see Morten Hørning Jensen, *Herod Antipas in Galilee: The Literary and Archaeological Sources on the Reign of Herod Antipas and Its Socio-Economic Impact on Galilee*, WUNT 2 215 (Tübingen, Germany: Mohr Siebeck, 2006).

threat because his ministry of healing was a sign of the in-breaking *reign of God*. Repentance was spiritual preparation for God's eschatological work of salvation.

Anyone familiar with the Jewish Scriptures knew that when God did act, he would not leave the rulers of this world unthreatened. This is what frightened Herod—the possibility that the advent of God's reign through Jesus might upset his own.[12]

Whether Herod believed that God was at work in Jesus is beside the point. Herod displays no fear of God. Power was Herod's god. What he feared was the hope that Jesus might give to the disinherited. A populace that believed that God was on the verge of breaking in was dangerous. Rome ramped up security every Passover because Passover always threatened to rekindle the memory of God's mighty act to save. It was precisely inasmuch as Jesus was obedient to his Father and rooted in the hopes and dreams of Israel that Jesus revealed himself to be a great danger to the rulers of his day.

There is a lesson here for Black Christians. Political relevance is not so far above us that we have to ask who will ascend and get it. It is not so low that we have to descend to the depths of the earth to retrieve it. The political relevance of the gospel message is in the stories and songs of Israel that make up the pages of the Old Testament. These are stories of a God who fights for us and against the enemies of his people. These are stories of a God who turns his compassionate eye toward those whom society forgets. Rome knew this and so did Herod.

What does Jesus say when he finds out that his mission has brought him into conflict with the sitting king of Israel? He says, "Go and tell that *fox* for me, 'Listen, I am casting out demons and performing

---

[12]I. Howard Marshall, *The Gospel of Luke: A Commentary on the Greek Text*, NIGTC (Grand Rapids, MI: Eerdmans, 1978), 570.

cures today and tomorrow, and on the third day I finish my work. Yet today, tomorrow, and the next day I must be on my way, because it is impossible for a prophet to be killed outside of Jerusalem'" (Lk 13:32-33, emphasis added).

Jesus' words show no deference to the political authority inherent in Herod's status. He calls him a fox. This is not a compliment. To be called a fox in Jesus' day meant being considered conniving and deceitful.[13] What about Herod might have led to Jesus calling him a fox? Herod Antipas did not maintain his rule over Galilee because the people believed him to be the rightful ruler, but because he had the backing of the empire.[14] His power was not real. His position was secured through posturing, compromise, and intrigue.[15] Insomuch as his concern was first and foremost his own survival and not the good of the people, the poor of Galilee could not look to him for succor.[16]

Herod was a fox, not a king. It is not even clear that he had the ability to carry out the threat levied against Jesus.[17] As a false power Herod Antipas had no say in reference to the work the Father had given Jesus to do. The point here, is that *fox* is not simply an analysis of Herod's limited piety. It is a description of his *political activity as it*

---

[13]Robert H. Stein, *Luke*, ed. E. Ray Clendenen and David S. Dockery, NAC 24 (Nashville: Broadman & Holman, 1992), 383; R. Alan Culpepper, "The Gospel of Luke," in *The Gospel of Luke–The Gospel of John*, NIB 9 (Nashville: Abingdon Press, 1995), 281.

[14]On Herod as "puppet ruler," see Joel Marcus, *Mark 1-8: A New Translation with Introduction and Commentary*, Anchor Bible (New York: Doubleday, 2000), 392.

[15]Herod does show some sympathy towards Jewish religious sensibilities, but there is no evidence that this was as a result of his own piety. Rather it was a means of keeping power. See Joel Marcus, "Herod Antipas," in *John the Baptist in History and Theology* (Columbia, SC: University of South Carolina Press, 2018), 98-112.

[16]Sakari Häkkinen, "Poverty in the First-Century Galilee," *Hervormde Teologiese Studies* 72, no. 4 (2016): 1-9.

[17]H. W. Hoehner, "Herod," in *The International Standard Bible Encyclopedia (Revised)*, ed. Geoffery W. Bromiley, Accordance electronic edition, version 1.2 (Grand Rapids, MI: Eerdmans, 1979), 695; R. Buth, "That Small-fry Herod Antipas, or When a Fox is Not a Fox," *Jerusalem Perspective* 40 (1993), argues that Herod's insignificance is the primary import of Jesus' fox language.

relates to the inevitable suffering of the people. This is a statement made in full view of Pharisees and sure to become a matter of public record.

How might Jesus' words inform a theology of the political witness of the church? Jesus shows that those Christians who have called out injustice are following in the footsteps of Jesus. Thus, when Frederick Douglass asked what to a slave is the Fourth of July, he had strong theological justification. When the Southern Christian Leadership Counsel took to the streets of Birmingham, Selma, and Memphis to speak openly about the sinfulness of the political landscape of its day, they were not far from Jesus and his statements about Herod the fox.

Jesus' words go beyond the dismissal of Herod to address the reception of prophets more generally. Jesus says that it is impossible for prophets to die outside of Jerusalem (Lk 13:33). His point is that there is a tradition of rejecting those God sends as messengers of his will. It is very easy to misunderstand Jesus' words about rejecting the prophets. We can assume that ancient Israel only rejected the "religious" message of the prophets not the things we deem political. But in Jesus' day there was a tradition that Isaiah the prophet had been killed in Jerusalem.[18] This justifies a brief discussion of Isaiah's message.

Isaiah is filled with messengers that offer a criticism of Israel both for its failure to follow the one true God and for its oppression of the poor:

- Ah, you who join house to house, / who add field to field, / until there is room for no one but you, / and you are left to live alone / in the midst of the land! (Is 5:8)

- Ah, sinful nation, / people laden with iniquity, / offspring who do evil, / children who deal corruptly, / who have forsaken the

---

[18]R. Alan Culpepper, "The Gospel of Luke," in *The Gospel of Luke–The Gospel of John*, NIB 9 (Nashville: Abingdon Press, 1995), 281.

LORD, / who have despised the Holy One of Israel, / who are utterly estranged! (Is 1:4)

- Learn to do good; / seek justice, / rescue the oppressed, / defend the orphan, / plead for the widow. (Is 1:17)

Isaiah was not rejected simply because he told Israel to worship Yahweh. He was rejected because Isaiah realized that true worship of Yahweh had implications for how one treated their neighbor. According to Isaiah, Israel's oppression of the poor in his day betrayed a practical apostasy.[19]

For Isaiah, piety must bear fruit in justice. Jesus knew that inasmuch as his message of justice impinged on the lives of the powerful, he was liable to rejection and death. Jesus not only embraced this prophetic tradition, he declared himself the climax of it by claiming that the acceptable day of the Lord (Is 61:1-2) had arrived in him (Lk 4:14-21).

Jesus' statement about Herod was not some spur of the moment criticism of a political figure that he did not like. Jesus saw his ministry as a part of a tradition of Israel's prophets who told the truth about unfaithfulness to God that manifested itself in the oppression of the disinherited. Jesus drew on the prophets as he spoke truth to power. Therefore, those Black Christians who see in those same prophets the warrant for their own public ministry have Jesus as their support.

PAUL, BRIEFLY CONSIDERED

Paul is often seen as the patron saint of the establishment, but this can only be maintained by paying attention to select portions of his corpus.[20] A holistic reading of Paul shows that he is willing to

---

[19]John D. W. Watts, *Isaiah 34–66*, WBC 25 (Grand Rapids, MI: Zondervan, 2005), 842-43.
[20]See Richard A. Horsley, ed., *Paul and Politics: Ekklesia, Israel, Imperium, Interpretation* (Harrisburg, PA: Trinity, 2000); for an overview of some recent political readings of Paul, see N. T. Wright, *Paul and His Recent Interpreters* (Minneapolis, MN: Fortress Press, 2015), 305-28.

critique authorities with vigor when necessary. Rather than a full examination of all the relevant Pauline passages, I will only consider a fleeting turn of phrase at the opening of Galatians.

Paul wrote his letter to the Galatians near the early portion of his writing career. He composed his letter to persuade a mixed congregation of Jewish and Gentile believers that faith in Christ was sufficient to make one a coheir to the promises made to Abraham and his ultimate heir the Messiah Jesus.[21] As a part of his opening address to the churches of Galatia, Paul says the following: "Grace to you and peace from God our Father and the Lord Jesus Christ, who gave himself for our sins to set us free from the present evil age, according to the will of our God and Father, to whom be the glory forever and ever. Amen" (Gal 1:3-5). When Paul speaks about Jesus giving himself for our sins he is more than capable of saying that it effects our justification (Rom 4:25) or that Jesus' death makes us heirs in Christ of all things (Rom 8:32). Here his emphasis is different. Jesus gave himself for our sins "to rescue us from the present evil age."

What does it mean for Paul to call the age evil? New Testament scholar Martyn notes that Paul believed that the world was under the domain of evil spiritual powers before the coming of the Messiah.[22] This is important because elsewhere in Paul's writings he suggests that these same "powers" hold sway over earthly leaders and rulers.[23] The political, economic, and social policies of unredeemed rulers, then, are a manifestation of evil powers that are opposed by

---

[21]Craig S. Keener, *Galatians: A Commentary* (Grand Rapids, MI: Baker Academic, 2019), 13-21.

[22]J. Louis Martyn, *Galatians: A Translation with Introduction and Commentary* (New Haven, CT: Yale University Press, 1997), 97.

[23]See the link between spiritual and material (human) powers in Ephesians 1:21 in Stephen E. Fowl's *Ephesians: A Commentary*, New Testament Library (Louisville, KY: Westminster John Knox Press, 2012), 60-61; and Charles H. Talbert's *Ephesians and Colossians*, Paideia Commentaries on the New Testament (Grand Rapids, MI: Baker Academic, 2007), 70.

God. These powers (along with the problem of human sin) are the enemies God sent his son to defeat. For this reason, our modern delineation between spiritual and political evil when read back into Paul's thought is an anachronism.

The "present evil age" can be understood to include the demonic evil of slavery in Rome and economic exploitation of the populace, both of which existed because of the policies of Roman leadership as dictated by spiritual forces.[24]

Most recognize that Paul's statement about the turning of the ages arises from his reading of that great Old Testament prophet Isaiah. Isaiah looks to the creation of a new heavens and a new earth after God changes the social and political lives of exiled Israel:

> Therefore thus says the Lord GOD:
> My servants shall eat,
>   but you shall be hungry;
> my servants shall drink,
>   but you shall be thirsty;
> my servants shall rejoice,
>   but you shall be put to shame. . . .
> For I am about to create new heavens
>   and a new earth;
> the former things shall not be remembered
>   or come to mind. (Is 65:13, 17)
>
> See, the former things have come to pass,
>   and new things I now declare;
> before they spring forth,
>   I tell you of them. (Is 42:9)

---

[24]Braxton makes it clear that whatever the nature of the evil, Paul's primary point is God's deliverance. Brad Ronnell Braxton, *No Longer Slaves: Galatians and the African American Experience* (Collegeville, MN: Liturgical Press, 2002), 62.

When Paul calls the present age evil and looks to the creation of a new one, he stands in the middle of the prophetic tradition. There are two dangers in evoking this tradition. We can flatten its message or underinterpret its implications. We can underinterpret it by saying that in Galatians Paul only has in mind "spiritual enslavement." Such a reading doesn't take into account how the transformed lives of believers changed the way that Christians lived in the world. Treating women equally, as called for in Galatians 3:28, would be a political act in an empire that had certain views about what a woman's place might be.[25] The second reading overinterprets Paul's meaning by assuming that it is the work of the church to establish God's kingdom on earth in its fullness now. We live as witnesses to the kingdom and voice our words of protest when the present evil age oversteps its bounds.

It might help to look at Colossians. In Colossians, Paul says that God calls us from the kingdom of darkness into the kingdom of the beloved son (Col 1:13). When Paul speaks about the kingdom of darkness he primarily has in mind the dark spiritual forces that torment the people of God.[26] As stated earlier, Paul believes that these dark powers also control earthly rulers. The economic, social, and political oppression of the people of God is nothing more than the physical manifestation of the spiritual sickness at the heart of the empire.

According to Paul, Jesus saves us from our sins, and he also calls us into a kingdom that treats its people better than the way Rome treats its citizens. When Paul calls this age *evil* and says that we are *rescued* from it, it is a statement that we are no longer bound to

---

[25]Beverly Roberts Gaventa, "Is Galatians Just a 'Guy Thing'?: A Theological Reflection," *Interpretation* 54, no. 3 (2000): 267-78.

[26]Edward Lohse, *Colossians and Philemon: A Commentary on the Epistles to the Colossians and to Philemon*, ed. Helmut Koester, trans. William R. Poehlmann and Robert J. Karris, Hermeneia 72 (Minneapolis, MN: Fortress Press, 1971), 37.

order our lives according to the priorities, values, and aims of this age. We are free to live differently while we await the coming of the true king. Calling the social and political order evil is a *political* assessment as well as a *theological* one. It is the assessment that Rev. Dr. King made in his critique of Jim Crow. King said that the current practices throughout the North and the South were a manifestation of the kingdom of darkness and that the kingdom of the beloved son called for a different way.

When Black Christians look upon the actions of political leaders and governments and call them *evil*, we are making a theological claim in the same way that Paul was. Protest is not unbiblical; it is a manifestation of our analysis of the human condition in light of God's own word and vision for the future. His vision may await an appointed time, but it is coming (Hab 2:1-4).

JOHN THE REVELATOR AND HIS VISIONS

The New Testament closes with a book that recounts the visions of John. These visions were sent to seven churches experiencing varying levels of persecution because of their fidelity to Jesus.[27] As it relates to the political witness of the church, I want to ask a simple question. What does John think of the Roman Empire?

John's clearest depiction of the empire comes in a vision of her eschatological fall in Revelation 18. Speaking of Rome's demise he says,

> Fallen, fallen is Babylon the great!
>> It has become a dwelling place of demons,
> a haunt of every foul spirit,
>> a haunt of every foul bird,
>>> a haunt of every foul and hateful beast. (Rev 18:2)

---

[27]See Brian K. Blount's *Can I Get a Witness: Reading Revelation Through African American Culture* (Louisville, KY: Westminster John Knox Press, 2005), 40-41.

In calling Rome Babylon he likens her to that great oppressive empire that conquered Israel.[28]

John, much like Paul, probably drew on Isaiah, who condemns ancient Babylon for the same reasons that John condemns Rome. Isaiah says,

> You will take up this taunt against the king of Babylon:
>> How the oppressor has ceased!
>>> How his insolence has ceased!
>> The LORD has broken the staff of the wicked,
>>> the scepter of rulers,
>> that struck down the peoples in wrath
>>> with unceasing blows,
>> that ruled the nations in anger
>>> with unrelenting persecution. (Is 14:4-6)

Earlier Isaiah calls Babylon a tyrant (Is 13:11). God judges Babylon for their pretensions to be in the place of God (Is 14:13) *and* for the resulting oppression of the nations and lands under its thumb. In the same way, John looks at the moral life of Rome and says that she is doomed for destruction.[29] This destruction is plainly the result of its socially and politically immoral culture.

John claims that rather than focusing on the flourishing of its people, Rome only cared about enriching itself.[30] This was seen particularly in its immoral sale of human beings. John, then, composed a letter read aloud to churches that condemns the economic policies inscribed in law (slavery). He says that these immoral activities along with persecution of Christians (Rev 18:24) will bring about God's eschatological judgement.

---

[28]David E. Aune, *Revelation 17–22*, WBC 52C (Grand Rapids, MI: Zondervan, 1998), 985.

[29]Robert H. Mounce, *The Book of Revelation*, rev. ed., NICNT (Grand Rapids, MI: Eerdmans, 1997), 326.

[30]Christopher C. Rowland, "The Book of Revelation," in *Hebrews–Revelation*, NIB 12 (Nashville: Abingdon Press, 1998), 696, says that Revelation 18 "gives a reader a glimpse of how the wealth of Babylon has been gained at the expense of millions."

The question that ought to keep Christians up at night is not the political activism of Black Christians. The question should be how 1 Timothy 2:1-4 came to dominate the conversation about the Christian's responsibility to the state. How did we manage to ignore the clearly political implications of Paul's casual remarks about the evil age in Galatians and his wider reflections on the links between evil powers and politicians? How did John's condemnation of Rome in Revelation fall from view?[31] Why did Jesus' public rebuke of Herod get lost to history? It may have been because it was in the best interest of those in power to silence Black voices. But if our voices are silenced the Scriptures still speak. But rather than leave it there, we conclude our reflections on the political witness of the church with a return to Jesus.

JESUS, PEACEMAKERS, AND PUBLIC WITNESS

Jesus' most famous address, known to history as the Sermon on the Mount, is recorded in Matthew 5–7. The mountain location echoes the giving of the law at Sinai. Just as the law was directed toward life in the Promised Land, Jesus' words are directed toward life in God's kingdom.[32] Jesus is the greater Moses because he does not simply repeat what he hears from God.[33] He speaks on his own accord as the divine king. If there is a place for the Christian to turn to for a way to witness in a world divided and torn by sin, this is it. I want to focus on what Jesus says about the desire for justice and the work of justice to his disciples.

---

[31]For a more extensive discussion of Revelation and politics, see Brian K. Blount's *Can I Get a Witness: Reading Revelation through African American Culture* (Louisville, KY: Westminster John Knox Press, 2005).

[32]Leon Morris, *The Gospel According to Matthew*, PNTC (Grand Rapids, MI: Eerdmans, 1992), 92.

[33]Although I do not agree that the Moses-Jesus exists in Matthew's Gospel to the extent that Allison does, Dale C. Allison, *The New Moses: A Matthean Typology* (Minneapolis, MN: Fortress Press, 1999) is a thorough study of the question.

We opened our reflections on the church's political witness with King's activities in Birmingham. His justification for his presence was simply that "injustice is here." He goes on to cite biblical characters who were moved to aid those in need. That leads to the question, Why did Paul or Isaiah or Amos care about justice?

Jesus explains what undergirds the actions of Paul, Isaiah, and Rev. Dr. King in two of his Beatitudes. He says, "Blessed are those who grieve, for they will be comforted. . . . Blessed are those who hunger and thirst for justice, for they will be filled" (Mt 5:4, 6, my translation). To mourn involves being saddened by the state of the world. To mourn is care. It is an act of rebellion against one's own sins and the sins of the world.[34]

A theology of mourning allowed Rev. Dr. King to look on the suffering of the people in Birmingham and refuse to turn away. Mourning calls on all of us to recognize our complicity in the sufferings of others. We do not simply mourn the sins of the world. We mourn our own greed, lusts, and desires that allow us to exploit others. Sin is more than exploitation, but it is certainly not less. A theology of mourning never allows us the privilege of apathy. We can never put the interests of our families or our country over the suffering of the world.

Mourning is intuition that things are not right—that more is possible. To think that more is possible is an act of political resistance in a world that wants us to believe that consumption is all there is. Our politicians run on our desires by convincing us that utopia is possible here and they alone can provide it.

The second Beatitude at the center of our reflections moves beyond the suspicion raised in our mourning. It articulates our hope: "Blessed are those who hunger and thirst for justice, for they

---

[34]Morris, *Gospel According to Matthew*, 97.

will be filled."[35] Hungering and thirsting for justice is nothing less than the continued longing for God to come and set things right. It is a vision of the just society established by God that does not waver in the face of evidence to the contrary. Mourning is not enough. We must have a vision for something different. Justice is that difference. Jesus, then, calls for a reconfiguration of the imagination in which we realize that the options presented to us by the world are not all that there is. There remains a better way and that better way is the kingdom of God. He wants us to see that his kingdom is something that is possible, at least as a foretaste, even while we wait for its full consummation. To hunger for justice is to hope that the things that cause us to mourn will not get the last word.

What does all of this have to do with the public witness of the church? Jesus asks us to see the brokenness in society and to artic- ulate an alternative vision for how we might live. This does not mean that we believe that we can establish the kingdom on earth before his second coming. It does mean that we see society for what it is: less than the kingdom. We let the world know that we see the cracks in the facade.

This call to hunger for justice, in the context of Jesus sitting on a mountain, must be understood as a messianic word:

> For a child has been born for us,
>> a son given to us;
> authority rests upon his shoulders;
>> and he is named

---

[35]Ulrich Luz, *Matthew 1–7: A Commentary on Matthew 1–7*, ed. Helmut Koester, trans. James E. Crouch, Hermeneia 61a (Minneapolis, MN: Fortress Press, 2007), 195, rightly questions whether we hunger for our personal righteousness or God's righteousness. This might be a false choice. To hunger for God's righteousness involves longing for his saving activity rooted in his trustworthiness. The result of that saving activity is a world filled with those who reflect his character in their moral behavior. See M. Eugene Boring, "The Gospel of Matthew," in *General Articles on the New Testament: Matthew–Mark*, NIB 8 (Nashville: Abingdon Press, 1995), 179.

Wonderful Counselor, Mighty God,
   Everlasting Father, Prince of Peace.
His authority shall grow continually,
   and there shall be endless peace
for the throne of David and his kingdom.
   He will establish and uphold it
with justice and with righteousness
   from this time onward and forevermore.
The zeal of the LORD of hosts will do this. (Is 9:6-7)

The messianic son of David, as the agent of God's will, would be known for establishing justice on the earth. To hunger for justice in a messianic context is to long for God to establish his just rule over the earth through his chosen king. Righteousness or justice then, is inescapably political. Hungering for justice is a hungering for the kingdom.

The two Beatitudes discussed above articulate the desire for justice. The last Beatitude under consideration is where Jesus provides us with the practices of justice. Matthew 5:9 says, "Blessed are the peacemakers, for they will be called the sons of God." Why make peace and how do we go about achieving it? Jesus calls his people to be *peacemakers* because the kingdom of the Messiah is one of peace. Again we have the vision of Isaiah:

His authority shall grow continually,
   and there shall be endless *peace*
for the throne of David and his kingdom.
   He will establish and uphold it
with justice and with righteousness
   from this time onward and forevermore.
The zeal of the LORD of hosts will do this. (Is 9:7, emphasis added)

The wolf shall live with the lamb,
   the leopard shall lie down with the kid,

the calf and the lion and the fatling together,
    and a little child shall lead them.
The cow and the bear shall graze,
    their young shall lie down together; . . .
They will not hurt or destroy
    on all my holy mountain;
for the earth will be full of the knowledge of the Lord
    as the waters cover the sea. (Is 11:6-9, emphasis added)

Isaiah envisions a kingdom in which the hostility between nations (Isaiah 9:7) and the created order will be removed (Is 11:1-9). To call God's people to peacemaking, then, means beginning the work of ending hostility that will mark the Messiah's reign. To claim that Jesus envisions the end of personal hostility and to neglect ethnic or national hostility does not do justice to the kingdom theology undergirding the entire sermon.[36]

What, then, does peacemaking involve and what does this have to do with the church's political witness? Biblical peacemaking is the cessation of hostilities between nations and individuals as a sign of God's in-breaking kingdom. Peacemaking involves assessing the claims of groups in conflict and making a judgment about who is correct and who is incorrect.

Peacemaking, then, cannot be separated from truth telling. The church's witness does not involve simply denouncing the excesses of both sides and making moral equivalencies. It involves calling injustice by its name. If the church is going to be on the side of *peace* in the United States, then there has to be an honest accounting of what this country has done and continues to do to Black and Brown people. Moderation or the middle ground is not always the loci of

---

[36]R. T. France, *The Gospel of Matthew*, NICNT (Grand Rapids, MI: Eerdmans, 2007), 169, says that the emphasis is "personal ethics." See instead Stott, *The Message of the Sermon on the Mount* (Downers Grove, IL: InterVarsity Press, 1978), 51.

righteousness. Housing discrimination has to be named. Unequal sentences and unfair policing has to be named. Sexism and the abuse and commodification of the Black female body has to end. Otherwise any peace is false and nonbiblical. Beyond naming there has to be some vision for the righting of wrongs and the restoration of relationships. The call to be peacemakers is the call for the church to enter the messy world of politics and point toward a better way of being human.

This peacemaking could be corporate, dealing with ethnic groups and nations at enmity, or it could be personal. When it is corporate, we are testifying to the universal reign of Jesus. When it is interpersonal, we are bearing witness to the work that God has done in our hearts. These things need not be put into competition.

The most interesting thing about this peacemaking is that it doesn't assume that those at enmity are believers. Jesus does not say make peace between Christians, but make peace. He doesn't say establish peace by making them Christians, but make peace. Why? Because peacemaking can be evangelistic. Through our efforts to bring peace we show the world the kind of king and kingdom we represent. The outcome of our peacemaking is to introduce people to the kingdom. Therefore the work of justice, when understood as direct testimony to God's kingdom, is evangelistic from start to finish. It is part (not the whole) of God's work of reconciling all things to himself.

CONCLUSION

At the heart of this chapter has been the desire to think through the church's interaction with the powers and rulers of our day. What is our responsibility? Much of the popular conversation on the Christian's duty focuses on the call to pray found in 1 Timothy 2:1-7 and the call to submit found in Romans 13:1-7. I have argued that neither of those passages, rightly understood, limits the Christian political witness, although it might inform the means. First Timothy 2:1-4 calls for prayer for all people, especially rulers. Timothy does not speak to what we might do when our convictions do not align with the empire. That same letter contains a criticism of a standing policy in Rome, namely slave trading (1 Tim 1:8-11). Romans 13:1-7 should be seen more as raising questions around theodicy and the negation of divinely sanctioned violence then a citadel against which no call for justice can prevail.

Turning to the wider New Testament witness, we looked at the testimony of Jesus. His criticism spoke to Herod's character *and* his politics. If Jesus could tell the Jews of his day that the leader of their country was corrupt, then why can't we? Paul's statement about the present evil age in Galatians also contains a rather unsubtle condemnation of the current political order. In much the same vein, John had strong words to say about Rome. We concluded with a return to Jesus' words and an examination of the Sermon on the Mount and its relationship to the political witness of the church.

The Black Christian, then, who hopes and works for a better world finds an ally in the God of Israel. He or she finds someone who does more than sympathize with our wants and needs. This God steps into history and reorders the universe in favor of those who trust in him. He calls us to enter into this work of actualizing the transformation he has already begun by the death and resurrection of his Son. This includes the work of discipleship, evangelism, and the pursuit of personal holiness. It also includes bearing witness to a different and better way of ordering our societies in a world whose default instinct is oppression. To do less would be to deny the kingdom.

FOUR

READING WHILE BLACK

THE BIBLE AND THE PURSUIT OF JUSTICE

■ ■ ■

The Government keeps lying to me telling me
that they come to set the people free.
KIRK FRANKLIN, "STRONG GOD"

He has brought down the powerful from their thrones,
and lifted up the lowly;
he has filled the hungry with good things,
and sent the rich away empty.
MARY, THE MOTHER OF JESUS (LUKE 1:52-53 NIV)

I WAS IN SEVENTH GRADE when I saw the movie *Malcolm X* starring Denzel Washington. That movie came out at a particular time in American history not so different from the one we inhabit. The war on drugs was in its twenty-first year with no end in sight. The crack epidemic was still rampaging through Black neighborhoods and families. I turned on the television and heard Black women referred to as "welfare queens" and Black men being accused of abandoning their families. They told me that food stamps encouraged laziness and that it was more likely that I would end up dead or in jail than with a college degree. The public depiction of blackness put its foot on our back in an attempt to stomp out Black dreams. But it was also an era of Black consciousness in which hip hop artists began to bring anti-violence messages into their songs and push for a positive understanding of what it meant to be Black in the United States.

Denzel Washington as Malcolm X came to us like a bolt of lightning. He was Black and proud and unapologetic in his demand for the freedom for our people. Denzel's portrayal was not the first time that I had come into contact with the Nation of Islam. Most weekends, there was a member of the Nation at a major intersection near my house selling their newspaper and talking to us about how the nation could give Black men a sense of respect. As a middle schooler, I knew very little about the actual teachings of the Nation of Islam. I knew that they seemed to care about what was happening to us. When *Malcolm X* came out when it did, it struck a chord with many Black boys and girls. Many in the Nation of Islam or other Black consciousness groups criticize Black Christians for following a religion that does so little for us.

Black members of other religions or Black secularists who critique Christianity because of its lack of concern for justice has followed Black Christians since the beginning. This is a part of the two-sided critique that the Black pastor has to deal with that I mentioned in chapter one. Not only must we push back on the European deconstruction of the Christian faith, we must also take seriously the claims coming from the Black critics.

I did not join the Nation of Islam for a variety of reasons, even when I most despaired of a hopeful future for African Americans in this country. Why? I came to believe that we must ask questions in their proper order. The fundamental question was whether or not the Christian story was true. I believed that the tomb was empty on the third day. White supremacy, even when practiced by Christians, cannot overcome the fact of the resurrection.

What about the justice that Black Christians desire? Are those who disdain the church correct that the Bible isn't up to the challenge of speaking to the issues of the day? Put simply, is the Bible a friend or foe in the Black quest for justice?

Some who maintain an ongoing but diminished role for the Scriptures suggest that the starting point for African American biblical exegesis is a *predetermined* definition of liberation that serves as the filter through which we examine the biblical texts to see if they meet our standard. The problem with this approach is that it assumes the *inspiration* and in effect *infallibility* of our current sociopolitical consensus and the inability of the biblical text to correct *us*. In other words, it displays a higher confidence in our wisdom than the wisdom of God's Word. As we stated in the introduction, biblical interpretation is not a one-sided monologue. The Black Christian brings his or her questions to the text and the text poses its own questions to us. We enter into a patient dialogue trusting that the fruit of such a discussion is good for our souls.

Stated differently, the Scriptures of the Old and New Testaments have a message of salvation, liberation, and reconciliation that itself *shapes* the African American Christian's vision of the present and the future. But things are not so simple. There have to be some points of connection between Black hopes and the Bible. We are not blank slates upon which the Scriptures can write anything. We come to these texts with our own experiences, hopes, and dreams. It would indeed be a tragedy if we encountered a Bible that told us that up was down, or that we are wrong to long for the freedom to work and raise families and not be harassed because of the color of our skin. It would be worse still if we encountered a God unconcerned with the strange fruit that grew upon the sycamore trees of the Jim Crow South. But I do not believe that the triune God revealed in the Old and New Testaments shows a lack of concern for Black lives or justice.

Will the evidence bear my assertion out? A full outline of the Bible's vision for the just society would be impossible. For the sake of space, I will limit myself to Luke's Gospel. I choose Luke because if it were the only book of the New Testament, it would be sufficient to validate my claim. The burden of this chapter, then, is to outline the ways in which the Gospel of Luke contains a vision for the just society transformed by the advent of God that speaks to the hearts of Black Christians. This chapter has two movements. Before we can address the Bible's vision for a just society, we must address the issue of Black cynicism about the Bible and the importance of the witness of our ancestors. In this first movement, I argue that Luke and Theophilus's identities, circumstances, and message contain unique points of contact with the Black experience. Their presence and witness matters for us in our day. Then I use Zechariah and Elizabeth to maintain that African Americans today might want to take the testimony of our forefathers and foremothers seriously. With that preparatory work done, the second movement examines the testimonies of Mary and her son, which directly address the hopes of Black Christians for justice.

LUKE, A GOSPEL WRITER FOR BLACK CHRISTIANS

Before we get to Luke's content, let's examine the significance of his existence. The circumstances surrounding the composition of Luke's Gospel contains interesting points of contact with the early Black encounter with Christianity. Luke is the only writer of the

New Testament texts who is probably Gentile.[1] He was most likely a convert from among the God-fearers who came to faith through the evangelistic witness of the apostles.[2]

In the wider culture, his status as a Gentile may have afforded him certain privileges that might have been denied to the Jewish people of his day. Nonetheless, his status as a Gentile within the early Christian circles was a matter of some controversy.[3] In the second volume of his work, Luke tells the story of how the church came to understand that both Jewish and Gentile believers were equal members of the people of God.

Luke's place in the canon is a testimony to God's value of all ethnic groups. According to Luke, the inclusion of the Gentiles was not an innovation cooked up by the early church in an attempt to increase its market share. Luke's Gospel argues that God always intended to create an international, multiethnic community for his own glory.

Luke the Gentile telling the story of God's plan for the reconciliation of all things in the Messiah Jesus is similar to the early generation of abolitionists and evangelists in the Black church. The African Methodist Episcopal Church began when Richard Allen and Absalom Jones demanded an *equal place* in the Methodist Episcopal Church and were refused.[4] In their preaching and teaching, just like

---

[1]R. Alan Culpepper, "The Gospel of Luke," in *The Gospel of Luke–The Gospel of John*, NIB 9 (Nashville: Abingdon Press, 1995), 9-10; François Bovon, *Luke 1: A Commentary on the Gospel of Luke 1:1–9:50*, ed. Helmut Koester, trans. Christine M. Thomas, Hermeneia 63a (Minneapolis, MN: Fortress Press, 2002), 8. Some contend that Luke was a Jewish follower of Jesus. See Isaac W. Oliver, *Torah Praxis after 70 CE: Pleading Matthew and Luke-Acts as Jewish Texts*, WUNT 2 355 (Tübingen, Germany: Mohr Siebeck, 2013). Rick Strelan makes a more audacious claim in *Luke the Priest: The Authority of the Author of the Third Gospel* (Abingdon, UK: Routledge, 2016). Even if he is Jewish, my point that he was trying to articulate the place of Gentiles within the larger purposes of God stands.

[2]John Nolland, *Luke 1–9:20*, WBC 35A (Grand Rapids, MI: Zondervan, 1989), xxxii.

[3]See Luke's own account of the resolution of this matter in Acts 15.

[4]Martha Simmons and Frank A. Thomas, *Preaching with Sacred Fire: An Anthology of African American Sermons 1750 to the Present* (New York: Norton and Norton, 2010), 105.

the Gospel writer Luke, these Black leaders argued that God's plan for the reconciliation of all things encompassed all people, including those of African descent:

> Oh thou God of all the nations upon the earth! We thank thee, that thou are no respecter of persons, and that thou hast made of one blood all nations of men. We thank thee, that thou hast appeared, in the fullness of time, in behalf of the nation from which most of the worshipping people now before thee, are descended. We thank thee, that the sun of righteousness has at last shed his morning beams upon them.[5]

Absalom Jones uses the language of fulfillment found both in the opening of Luke's Gospel (Lk 1:1-4) and the letters of Paul (Gal 4:4-7) to speak about the gospel coming to those of African descent.[6] Their conversion, according to Absalom, is no afterthought after God's original plan went astray. According to Absalom, God's plan is revealed in all its glory *in the conversion of African men and women.* Jones, then, comes close to Luke whose whole goal in writing Luke–Acts was to show that God's plan was always for the nations to know, worship, and obey the Messiah.[7]

Luke writing as a Gentile to other Gentiles to tell them that they have a place in God's kingdom is of direct relevance to Black preachers who proclaim to their congregations that they have a place in the kingdom of God as sons and daughters. This place as

---

[5]Simmons and Thomas, *Preaching with Sacred Fire*, 75.

[6]Luke 1:1 says, "Many have undertaken to draw up an account of the things that have been *fulfilled* among us." See also Galatians 4:4-5, which says, "But when the set time had *fully come*, God sent his Son, born of a woman, born under the law, to redeem those under the law, that we might receive adoption to sonship," (emphasis added).

[7]Stephanie Buckhanon Crowder, "Luke," in *True to Our Native Land: An African American New Testament Commentary* (Minneapolis, MN: Fortress Press, 2007), 158, says, "The events have not only taken place but have been fulfilled. . . . Thus the writer indicates a historical-theological underpinning for what has occurred." Stated differently, history and theology rightly merge in Luke's account.

sons and daughters in God's kingdom trumps any attempt by lesser kingdoms to make us second-class citizens. We are God's children. The United States (or any other country) has no say in determining our value.

Luke, then, a Gospel writer who links the conversion of Gentiles to God's wider purposes, can be seen as something of a patron saint of African American ecclesial interpretation. That this story takes up some one quarter of the New Testament is not without consequence.[8] One might be tempted to say that the place of all ethnicities in the kingdom of God is a bright red line running right down the middle of the New Testament.

LUKE, THEOPHILUS, AND THE THINGS
WE HAVE BEEN TAUGHT

Luke addresses his Gospel to someone named Theophilus. Most agree that he was a real person, not a stand in for Christian Gentiles.[9] Luke's motivation for writing to Theophilus might also speak to the concerns of Black Christians. Luke says,

> Since many have undertaken to set down an orderly account of the events that have been fulfilled among us, just as they were handed on to us by those who from the beginning were eyewitnesses and servants of the word, I too decided, after investigating everything carefully from the very first, to write an orderly account for you, most excellent Theophilus, so that you may know the truth concerning the things about which you have been instructed. (Lk 1:1-4)

Luke wants Theophilus to have certainty about the things that he has been taught about Jesus. It seems that Theophilus's first encounter

---

[8]Luke Timothy Johnson, *The Gospel of Luke*, Sacra Pagina (Collegeville, MN: Liturgical Press, 1991), 1.

[9]Johnson, *Gospel of Luke*, 1

with the gospel was not through the written word, but through the work of evangelists and teachers. Here he is close to the conversion of enslaved African Americans whose first conversions in large numbers came through the preaching witness of evangelists during the revivals of the great awakenings.[10] Nonetheless, there was a question of whether the Christianity that the enslaved were taught was indeed the Christianity of the Bible. Professor Allen Dwight Callahan quotes an early catechism used to teach slaves. It read:

> Who gave you a master and a mistress?
> God gave them to me.
> Who says that you must obey them?
> God says that I must.
> What book tells you these things?
> The Bible.[11]

Early Black conversion entailed finding the real Jesus among the false alternatives contending for power in the culture. Theophilus was not a slave being told that Jesus wants him to obey his masters as unto the Lord. But Luke does mention the fact that other accounts of Jesus were floating around that may not have been helpful.

We do not know which accounts Luke has in mind. Some assume Luke finds fault in the canonical Gospels.[12] This seems hard to accept given that he uses Mark as a basis for much of his work. Although there are clearly different emphases, it would be going beyond the evidence to see Mark and Luke as being in fundamental conflict.[13] So whatever gospel Luke corrects, it is not synoptic testimony nor is it

---

[10]On a slave's aural encounter with the Bible and mass conversion see Allen Dwight Callahan, *The Talking Book: African Americans and the Bible* (New Haven, CT: Yale University Press, 2006), 4, 12.

[11]Callahan, *Talking Book*, 32.

[12]Johnson, *Gospel of Luke*, 30.

[13]See Joel Green, *The Gospel of Luke*, NICNT (Grand Rapids, MI: Eerdmans, 1997), 37.

the gospel of John, which has yet to be written. Therefore, as an alternative to potentially misleading pictures of Jesus, Luke's Gospel meets the early experience of Black Christians whose Bible reading awakened them to the truth about God. But if Luke is the Gospel writer for Black Christians, the question remains: What did he have to say?

ZECHARIAH AND ELIZABETH AS THE VINDICATION OF BLACK HOPE

Matthew and Luke are the only Gospels that recount the events surrounding the birth of Jesus. Luke does not open with Christ's nativity. Jesus and his family begin offstage, and we start with an elderly couple: Zechariah and Elizabeth. Luke gives us precious few details about them, but it is enough to sketch something of their lives and their relevance to the hopes and aspirations of Israel in their day and Black Christians in ours. Luke tells us that Zechariah was a priest and Elizabeth descended from a priestly family. For Zechariah, this meant that apart from his annual trips to Jerusalem, much of his year was spent teaching, investigating issues of purity, and interceding for the people (Lev 10:10-11).[14] Elizabeth would have been raised in a family that did the same.

Zechariah and Elizabeth, then, were directly involved in making *theological* sense of Israel's status as oppressed people under the thumb of the Roman Empire. They would have faced the cynicism and despair that marks the lives of the disinherited. They interacted with people every day whose whole lives and the lives of their grandparents had been shaped by foreign rule and the casual disdain that accompanied it. They would have faced the same questions that Black pastors have had to deal with for generations. Where is God?

---

[14]C. Fletcher-Louis, "Priests and Priesthood," in *Dictionary of Jesus and the Gospels*, ed. Joel B. Green, Jeannine K. Brown, and Nicholas Perrin, 2nd ed. (Downers Grove, IL: InterVarsity Press, 2013), 697.

Why hasn't he saved us? Does he care about our suffering? Zechariah must have been forced to explain what Torah faithfulness meant in his context. Why keep the festivals and say the prayers if tomorrow might look much the same as yesterday?

Howard Thurman in discussing the relationship between Christianity and the oppressed notices the following:

> I can count on the fingers of one hand the number of times that I have heard a sermon on the meaning of religion, of Christianity, to the man who stands with his back against the wall. It is urgent that my meaning be made crystal clear. The masses of men live with their backs constantly against the wall. They are the poor, the disinherited, the dispossessed. What does our religion say to them?[15]

It is not too much of an interpretive leap to say that much of Judea lived with its back against the wall. Zechariah's son would address a community dealing with life as the disinherited (Lk 3:10-14). John knew about corrupt tax collectors and exploitative soldiers. Could he have learned about the biblical critique of such things through the teaching of his mother and father? It is impossible to imagine that Zechariah and Elizabeth would be uninformed about the hard questions posed to religious leaders about poverty, oppression, faith, and hope in the God of Israel.

Nonetheless, Zechariah and Elizabeth were "righteous before God, walking in all the commandments and ordinances of the Lord blamelessly" (Lk 1:5, my translation). They had walked from one end of their life to the other and maintained their faith in God despite the fact that many of their friends and neighbors may have long since given up any hope that God might act. They continued in this faith even though they had been unable to conceive and give birth to a child.

---

[15]Howard Thurman, *Jesus and the Disinherited* (Boston: Beacon Press, 1976), 3.

Zechariah and Elizabeth lived with national (Israel under the rule of Rome) and personal (no children) tragedy. In Luke's Gospel, they represent all Israelites whose personal stories carry the brokenness of the larger corporate narrative within them. Similarly, Black suffering from injustice is not simply corporate; it is deeply personal. It invades the homes, bedrooms, schools, churches, and delivery rooms of Black families.

Zechariah and Elizabeth are, in a sense, Israel writ small. Elizabeth and Zechariah's generation could say alongside Jeremiah's, "The harvest is past, the summer has ended, and we are not saved" (Jer 8:20). It is important that Luke begins here because it situates the Jesus story in the middle of the pain of Israel, which includes the large-scale tragedy of exile and disinheritance along with the personal traumas each individual Israelite must face. In other words, Luke begins with the issue of injustice as a central concern.

Elizabeth and Zechariah are crucial for understanding Black hope. As the faithful elderly who persevered in the faith despite long-delayed hope, they are our Black grandparents who dragged us to church and prayed for us when we lacked the faith to pray for ourselves. But more urgently, Zechariah and Elizabeth are the first generation of Black Christians who came to faith during slavery. Why put your faith in the God worshiped by slave owners? What good could come of it? How could its message be of use to you? The question posed by Frederick Douglass could also be found in the lament psalms of Israel: "Does a righteous God govern the universe? And for what does he hold the thunders in his right hand if not to smite the oppressor, and deliver the spoiled out of the hand of the spoiler?"[16]

---

[16]Frederick Douglass, *The Life of an American Slave* (Boston: Anti-Slavery Office, 1845), 77-82; Milton C. Sernett, ed., *African American Religious History: A Documentary Witness* (Durham, NC: Duke University Press, 1999), 105.

Why would such a people who have every reason for cynicism put their faith in a God whose promises seem long delayed? The answer that Zechariah and Elizabeth provided is *memory*. When faced with the delay of redemption, they remembered. Luke speaks of those in their generation who were looking for "the consolation of Israel" (Lk 2:25). The phrase "consolation of Israel" comes from Isaiah 40. The latter portions of Isaiah repeatedly speak of a second exodus in which Israel would again be free. The first exodus served as the basis for the hope of a second act of God's redemption. John, their son, would articulate the same hope for a new exodus. That is why his ministry would take place near the Jordan—that locale through which God opened a way into the Promised Land. The exodus, then, was a focus of hope for his family.[17]

Why did Zechariah and Elizabeth continue to trust in God? Because he was a God who frees from slavery—his fundamental character as *liberator* marked him out as trustworthy, even when they had yet to experience it. Black Christians who came to Christ surrounded by the false Gospel given to them by their slave masters were right to see in the *exodus narrative* a God worthy of their trust. The first generation of Black Christians and Zechariah's generation share a common faith in the God revealed during the exodus. *Therefore* God's decision to visit Zechariah and Elizabeth and Luke's decision to begin his story here are in themselves vindications of Black faithfulness because we too know the longing for consolation.

In wider scope of the Bible, God's decision to allow Elizabeth to give birth to a son is not impressive. We have read that story before. The child of promise, Isaac, was born of a woman long past birthing

---

[17]While we might associate the exodus with the crossing of the Red Sea, the biblical evocation of "the exodus" extended from the departure from Egypt through to their entry into the Promised Land. The baptism by the Jordan was a "passing through the water" that preceded a fresh reception of God's promises.

age. But that is the point. God has not changed. In Luke's opening chapter God is playing his greatest hits, so to speak, reminding Israel of who they serve.

This miracle of John's birth spread like a virus of hope infecting the bloodstream of Israel, causing many to ponder, "What then will this child become?" (Lk 1:66). It is true that not every family received a child after years of suffering; it is also true that many in Israel died never having tasted freedom from Egypt. They lived and died as the enslaved. But the exodus put the suffering of the enslaved dead in a new light. It showed that their suffering was not in vain because God remembered. God's memory also raises the possibility, in the grand scope of history, of the resurrection.[18] If the God of Israel could defeat the gods of Egypt, might he defeat death itself so that all might share in the promised inheritance (Ezek 37:1-14)?[19] God's acts of redemption work forward and backward, throwing fresh light on all our stories.

The early Black Christians also looked backward to make sense of their stories. Daniel Alexander Payne, that early AME bishop, when speaking of the emancipation of enslaved persons in Washington, DC, said, "If we ask, who has sent us this great deliverance? The answer shall be, the Lord . . . the God of Abraham and Isaac, and Jacob. . . . For the oppressed and enslaved of all peoples, God has raised up, and will continue to raise up, his Moses and Aaron."[20] According to Payne, Black freedom did not arise from the charity of presidents but from the sovereign hand of God. Just like the story of the exodus in

---

[18]Jesus makes this very argument in his debates with his opponents. He says, "And as for the resurrection of the dead, have you not read what was said to you by God, 'I am the God of Abraham, the God of Isaac, and the God of Jacob'? He is God not of the dead, but of the living" (Mt 22:31-32).

[19]See Jesus' own argument along these lines in Mt 23:32.

[20]Daniel Alexander Payne, "Welcome to the Ransomed," in *African American Religious History: A Documentary Witness*, ed. Milton C. Sernett (Durham, NC: Duke University Press), 236.

the lives of Zechariah and Elizabeth, the liberation of the enslaved persons in DC works backward (vindicating past faith in God) and forward (providing hope for the liberation of all slaves).

The testimonies of Zechariah, Elizabeth, and the early Black believers challenge us. It is easy to claim that their faith was rooted in a simple-minded belief in a better future that gave them comfort and release from the hopelessness that marked the Jim Crow era and slavery. But are things so simple? Is it possible that they gained a hard-won confidence in God by reflecting on the biblical stories of God's faithfulness in the past *and* by seeing that same God active in their own lives? Is their faith, seemingly vindicated by the advent of God to liberate them, a counter to our cynical claim that God has not done enough? Does Black freedom and the fits and starts of Black progress call us to wonder like those Israelites gathered around Zechariah and Elizabeth what this *child* might be? For Zechariah and Elizabeth the miracle child is John. For the African American Christian the miracle is the Black church born of truly miraculous circumstances and whose witness to Jesus has served as something of a forerunner preparing America to accept a truer and fuller gospel.

Zechariah and Elizabeth function in Luke's narrative as a reminder that a dream deferred is not a dream denied. In the same way, the faith of the Black church, the grandmothers and the grandfathers among us, challenges us to go beyond nostalgia for an era of faith long past. We must do more than say thank you. We must consider again the things of God and wonder what their testimony means for us.

THE TESTIMONY OF MARY AND THE HOPE OF EVERY BLACK CHRISTIAN

If the collective faith of Black grandmothers and grandfathers challenges us to reconsider the faith, the question remains as to what faith we are to reconsider. What kind of God do we encounter in the gospel of Luke? What does the coming of Jesus mean for Black folks on the other side of the Civil War, Jim Crow, the Civil Rights Movement, and our first Black president?

We begin with the testimony of Mary. She was, as we know, a young girl on the verge of an unremarkable but potentially joyful life as the spouse of a man (Joseph) who by all accounts loved her deeply (Mt 1:18-19). Nazareth, Mary's hometown, was a settlement of some two hundred souls about an hour's walk from Sepphoris, the former district capital of Galilee. It was also located near one of the major trade routes of the empire. Those traveling from Egypt to Damascus would pass by their hometown.[21]

It is wrong to imagine that Mary and Joseph lived in some idyllic farm town far from the politics of the day. Joseph and Mary grew up in the shadow of the empire with the reminder of Rome's domination just a short jaunt down the road. Whatever dreams that Mary nursed in her teenage heart about her future were forever changed by a visit from the angel Gabriel. He let her know that she would not simply be a witness to what God might do in the world; she would be a participant. She would be the loci of the tabernacling of God (Jn 1:14) as the Spirit of God knit together the hope of the world in her womb (Lk 1:35).

For some, this reading of the Lukan story, with such a strong affirmation of the virgin birth, taken at face value smacks of sentimentalism or, even worse, fundamentalism. As we have said earlier, if Black biblical interpretation is to be free to chart its own path, it is also free to reject the thoroughgoing skepticism that stands as one

---

[21]R. Riesner, "Archeology and Geography," in *Dictionary of Jesus and the Gospels*, ed. Joel B. Green, Jeannine K. Brown, and Nicholas Perrin, 2nd ed. (Downers Grove, IL: InterVarsity Press, 2013), 49.

legacy of the European dominance of biblical studies. Behind the skepticism about the virgin birth lies a whole tradition of skepticism about the nature of God's involvement in human affairs. Once we posit a Creator, which is the bedrock of all Jewish and Christian theological reflection, then all things become possible. Building on the words of St. Paul, "Why is it thought incredible by any of you that God raises the dead?" (Acts 26:8). Why can't God enable a virgin birth? It will not do to mention the lack of early attestation of the birth as if a Markan birth account would sway opinion. Others must own their skepticism and I my trust, both of which arise out of deeply held convictions about the nature of reality.

To return to Nazareth, we encounter Mary being asked to give the entirety of herself to give birth to a son who would change the world in ways that she could not imagine. In this very risk, this yes to God, Mary stands in for Black (and all other) Christians who are called to give the entirety of themselves, their very bodies for a future that they cannot see. Mary is the patron saint of faithful activists who give their very bodies as witnesses to God's saving work.

But what did Mary think about these things? What did she think that God had ushered in through his choice of her as the one to bring his son into the world?

Mary's song (Lk 1:46), known to history by the opening words in Latin, the *Magnificat,* begins with a word of praise: "My soul magnifies the Lord." These words are important because they locate Mary squarely within the faith of Israel. Mary was a believer and a worshiper. Her song is more than a statement about political liberation. Her testimony includes the worship of the one true God. Political liberation (to use a modern dichotomy alien to the first century) had as its telos the liberty to worship, not merely an assertion of their own political vision.

But why does Mary worship the one God of Israel? She worships God because he is a merciful God who does not respect money or power or influence but turns his loving attention toward all who fear him (Lk 1:50). Mary further rejoices that "He has shown strength with his arm; / he has scattered the proud in the thoughts of their hearts" (Lk 1:51 NIV). This means that the proud who devise plans to shape the world to cater to their pleasure discover that

He has brought down the powerful from their thrones,
    and lifted up the lowly;
he has filled the hungry with good things,
    and sent the rich away empty.
He has helped his servant Israel,
    in remembrance of his mercy. (Lk 1:52-54)

Is this not the hope of every Black Christian, that God might hear and save? That he might look upon those who deny us loans for houses or charge exorbitant interest rates in order to cordon us off into little pockets of poverty and say to them your oppression has been met with the advent of God? This is Mary's claim, that God reveals himself in glory by turning his attention towards those that the world deems unworthy and lifting them up to a place of honor.

Mary uses a phrase in her description of God that supports our claim about God's pleasure in liberating a people to worship him. She says that he has shown "strength with his arm." This is drawn from Isaiah and his prediction of a second exodus:

Awake, awake, put on strength,
    O arm of the LORD!
Awake, as in days of old,
    the generations of long ago! . . .
Was it not you who dried up the sea,
    the waters of the great deep;

who made the depths of the sea a way
    for the redeemed to cross over? (Is 51:9-10, emphasis added)

Isaiah calls on the God of the exodus to work a second miracle and call his exiled people home. This same idea is picked up a little later in Isaiah, when he speaks about a revelation of God's glory for all the world to see:

The Lord has bared his holy arm
    before the eyes of all the nations;
and all the ends of the earth shall see
    the salvation of our God.
    Depart, depart, go out from there! . . .
For you shall not go out in haste,
    and you shall not go in flight;
for the Lord will go before you,
    and the God of Israel will be your rear guard. (Is 52:10-12)

The careful reader of Isaiah will note that Isaiah goes on from here to describe a suffering servant whose death for sins brings about a second exodus and the end of the covenant curses that led to Israel's exile (Is 52:13–53:12). When Mary speaks about the revelation of *God's arm*, she evokes the image of the *exodus* and the end of *slavery*. Israel learned something fundamental about God in the exodus event. He is the God who liberates. When they looked forward to what God might do in the future, they looked back to the exodus event and said that whatever happened it had to be in keeping with that revelation of God's character. In that story God acted to free a people from slavery, not as an end of itself, but so that the newly liberated people might testify to a different way of being human. God gave Israel freedom and a vocation.

Mary claims that through her child God would again liberate his people. He would bare his arm. But how far did Mary see? Did she read further into Isaiah and ponder the fate of the servant? Did she return to Isaiah when Simeon told her that a sword would pierce her soul too (Lk 2:33–35)? We may never know. We do know that Mary's imagery of the arm of the Lord and the exodus it evokes touches on that historic link between African Americans and the God of the Bible. The exodus is fundamental and in it Black Christians found a God who grants us liberation and a whole life to live before him.

What is the testimony of Mary? The testimony of Mary is that even in the shadow of the empire there is a space for hope and that sometimes in that space, God calls us from the shadows to join him in his great work of salvation and liberation.

This liberation, at least as described in Isaiah, might have to pass through suffering and death. Mary might have been more prophetic than she knew. However this freedom came, it would arrive at the expense of those who exalted themselves over against the weak and God their champion. It is vital that Mary didn't look down the long hall of history and construct a God to suit the imaginations of enslaved Black people longing for freedom. Such a God was already there waiting for Mary and us. Mary, when she came face to face with this God, was left with little else to do but worship. It is not surprising that our foremothers and fathers did the same.

THE BAPTISM OF THE SON AND THE HOPE
OF THE DISINHERITED (LUKE 3:21-22)

We first encounter Jesus when he is about to be baptized by John near the Jordan river. As stated earlier, anyone with a passing knowledge of the great stories of Israel couldn't miss the point of the location: the same God who acted to liberate his people from Egypt was on the verge of another great work. John and Jesus' ministry takes place in the shadow of the exodus, and therefore the Black hermeneutical practice of highlighting the exodus is thereby vindicated. God did not choose the Egyptians. He chose the enslaved and this is the story evoked as Jesus begins his ministry.

What does God tell us at Jesus' baptism? He calls Jesus "my Son, the Beloved" and says, "With you I am well pleased" (Lk 3:22). Recognizing Jesus as Son speaks to Black concerns for justice because sonship is linked to kingship and righteous rule. Once we agree that Jesus is the Son of God and Israel's true king, the next question becomes, What kind of king will he be? What are the key facets of his rule?

Kingship in the Bible is linked to justice. We see this in the royal psalms (Ps 72:1-4). According to the Psalmist, the king—who reflects God's own justice—is on the side of the poor and disinherited. Jesus' kingly sonship is inseparable from God's justice because Israel's king cares for the poor.

The rest of Luke's Gospel will reveal that Jesus is not Son merely because he is king like all the other kings of Israel. He is *Son* because he shares in the divine identity of the Father that precedes the creation of the world.[22]

THE SERMON OF THE SON (LUKE 4:15-20)

Following Jesus' baptism, he is led by the Spirit into the wilderness to be tempted by Satan. We are again in the world of the exodus. When Israel is tested in the wilderness, she fails and abandons the God who saves (Ex 32:1-17). Jesus, by contrast, remains true to God by showing his commitment to the Scriptures (Lk 4:1-13). Three times Jesus responds to Satan's temptation by quoting Deuteronomy, the text given to Israel on the verge of their entry into the Promised

---

[22]C. Kavin Rowe, *Early Narrative Christology: The Lord in the Gospel of Luke* (Berlin: Walter de Gruyter, 2006).

Land. By citing Deuteronomy, Jesus sets the stage for his first sermon in Nazareth to be heard as the greater law. They are words for the formerly enslaved on the verge of receiving God's promises.

One more point needs to be made here as it specifically relates to Black Christian biblical interpretation. In chapter one, I argued that all theology is canonical in that everyone who attempts to think about the Bible must place the variety of biblical texts in some kind of order, understanding one in light of others. This isn't unique to Black Christians; everyone does it.

The question isn't always which account of Christianity uses the Bible. The question is which does justice to as much of the biblical witness as possible. There are uses of Scripture that utter a false testimony about God. This is what we see in Satan's use of Scripture in the wilderness. The problem isn't that the Scriptures that Satan quoted were untrue, but when made to do the work that he wanted them to do, they distorted the biblical witness. This is my claim about the slave master exegesis of the antebellum South. The slave master arrangement of biblical material bore false witness about God. This remains true of quotations of the Bible in our own day that challenge our commitment to the refugee, the poor, and the disinherited.

But we have wandered far from the wilderness of first-century Judea. Luke's point is plain enough. Jesus triumphs where corporate Israel failed. Following this victory over temptation in the wilderness, Jesus arrives in Nazareth and delivers his first sermon. Jesus stands to read in the synagogue, and he is given the scroll for the prophet Isaiah. Providence had this book as the assigned text, but Jesus chose which portion of text to read.[23] Luke records a conflation of Isaiah 61:1 and Isaiah 58:6. Isaiah 61:1 speaks about the servant of YHWH

---

[23]R. Alan Culpepper, "The Gospel of Luke," in *The Gospel of Luke–The Gospel of John*, NIB 9 (Nashville: Abingdon Press, 1995), 105.

who has reappeared throughout Isaiah 40–66 (42:1-9; 49:1-7; 52:13–53:12). In this passage, the servant states his God-given mission:

> The spirit of the Lord GOD is upon me,
>> because the LORD has anointed me;
> he has sent me to bring good news to the oppressed,
>> to bind up the brokenhearted,
> to proclaim liberty to the captives,
>> and release to the prisoners. (Is 61:1)

Isaiah 58:6, also alluded to by Jesus during his sermon, occurs in the context of God's critique of the false religiosity of Israel:

> "Why do we fast, but you do not see?
>> Why humble ourselves, but you do not notice?"
> Look, you serve your own interest on your fast day,
>> and oppress all your workers. . . .
> Is such the fast that I choose,
>> a day to humble oneself?
> Is it to bow down the head like a bulrush,
>> and to lie in sackcloth and ashes?
> Will you call this a fast,
>> a day acceptable to the Lord?
> Is not this the fast that I choose:
>> to loose the bonds of injustice,
>> to undo the thongs of the yoke,
> to let the oppressed go free,
>> *and to break every yoke*? (Is 58:3, 5-6, emphasis added)

What do these two texts as the central pillars of Jesus' ministry mean for Black Christians? First, Jesus preaches the gospel to the *poor*, the brokenhearted are healed, and those in bondage are set free. This shows that those whom society has declared secondary receive the place of priority in the kingdom. In a society where Black lives have historically been undervalued, we can know that we have an advocate in the person of Christ.

This theme of God's value of the undervalued, highlighted by Jesus, runs right through the New Testament. Paul speaks about it when he says, "God chose what is low and despised in the world, things that are not, to reduce to nothing things that are" (1 Cor 1:28).[24] James argues much the same in his letter when he says, "Listen, my beloved brothers and sisters. Has not God chosen the poor in the world to be rich in faith and to be heirs of the kingdom that he has promised to those who love him?" (Jas 2:5).

Jesus' reading of the Israelite prophetic tradition becomes paradigmatic for the church. Isaiah 61:1, as a central pillar of Jesus' ministry philosophy, tells the Black Christian that neither slavery nor Jim Crow nor housing discrimination, nor loan discrimination nor any other weapon influences God's love for them. In fact, it is just the opposite. God displays his glory precisely in rejecting the value systems posed by the world. It is the rejection of the world's evaluation that lifts the soul of the Black Christian because this country has repeatedly claimed that Blacks are ontologically inferior.

It is important to point out that the "gospel" preached here and elsewhere does more than affirm the value of the poor. Jesus sees them as *moral agents* capable of repentance. Stated differently, it is often stated that "good news" for the poor is bread or a job or political freedom. That is true insofar as it goes. But Jesus also cared about the *spiritual lives* of the poor. He saw them as bodies and souls. His call to repent acknowledges the fact that their poverty doesn't remove their agency. The poor are capable of sin and repentance. Repentance means that even if they remain poor, they can do so as

---

[24]It is important to note that these people are not actually lowly or despised by God, but rather society doesn't value them.

different people. The enslaved recognized this. We see this on page after page of their testimony. Yes, they longed for actual freedom (no excessive spiritualization here) but they also rejoiced in the change wrought in their lives by the advent of God.

The second Isaiah allusion included in Jesus' first sermon (Is 58:6) prevents us from too much focus on the poor as moral agents to the exclusion of the fact that they are actually poor. Isaiah 58:1-6 lambastes a fake religiosity more concerned with ritual than transforming the lived situation of the poor. According to Isaiah, true practice of religion ought to result in concrete change, the breaking of yokes. He does not mean the occasional private act of liberation, but "to break the chains of injustice." What could this mean other than a transformation of the structures of societies that trap people in hopelessness? Jesus has in mind the creation of a different type of world.

Jesus' ministry and the kingdom that he embodies involves nothing less than the creation of a new world in which the marginalized are healed spiritually, economically, and psychologically. The wealthy, inasmuch as they participate in and adopt the values of a society that dehumanizes people, find themselves opposing the reign of God. This dehumanization can take two forms. First, it can treat the poor as mere bodies that need food and not the transforming love of God. Second, it can view them as souls whose experience of the here and now should not trouble us.[25] This is false religion that has little to do with Jesus.

CONCLUSION

The Black Christian is often beset from the left and the right. Those on the right too often contend that the Bible speaks to their souls

---

[25]See Ibram X. Kendi, *Stamped from the Beginning: The Definitive History of Racist Ideas in America* (New York: Nation Books, 2016), 47-57.

and not the liberation of their bodies. Those on the left maintain that those on the right are correct. The Bible doesn't clearly address the needs of Black and Brown folks. Therefore, it must either be supplemented or replaced. I am not claiming that the Bible outlines the policies necessary for the proper functioning of a Democratic Republic. I am saying that it outlines the basic principles and critiques of power that equip Black Christians for their life and work in these United States.

FIVE

BLACK AND PROUD

THE BIBLE AND BLACK IDENTITY

■ ■ ■

I am black and beautiful, O daughters of Jerusalem.

SONG OF SOLOMON 1:1[1]

Say it loud! I'm black and I'm proud!

JAMES BROWN

A FUNDAMENTAL CRITICISM of Black Christianity is that it is an alien thing, an imposition of the white man through the persuasive power of the whip and the chain. The first encounter with Jesus, we are told, came from those who wanted us docile and accepting of our earthly status while we waited for succor in the world to come. Black Christianity, for some, is an oxymoron because the Christian story is not ours. We are latecomers to a drama written by others. There are two ways to answer this question, one biblical and the other historical. We will consider the historical issues before moving on to the much

---

[1]For a full defense of the black and beautiful translation, see Renita J. Weems, "The Song of Songs," in *Introduction to Wisdom Literature: Proverbs–Sirach*, NIB 5 (Nashville: Abingdon Press, 1997), 382-84.

more important discussion of the Bible and ethnic identity, which will take up the bulk of this chapter.

Historically, the claim that Christianity is European is fundamentally false. This can easily be proved by anyone with access to a history book and a map. It is a fact hiding in plain sight that the three major centers of early Christianity were the patriarchs of Rome, Antioch, and Alexandria.[2] Of these three only Rome is in what we call Western Europe. Alexandria is located in Egypt, a major early center of African culture. We do not have firm information on how Christianity came to North Africa, but tradition has it that it was evangelized by St. Mark.[3] From this North African church comes some of the greatest minds that Christianity has produced, such as Augustine and Tertullian.

Those who doubt the blackness of early Christianity are going to have to make a decision. Either some Westerners have whitewashed Egyptian history by turning many of its characters into Europeans, or they have not. If they have whitewashed Egyptian history, then that whitewashing extends to the era of the early church. This means that the leading lights of early Christianity were Black and Brown folks or Egypt isn't as African as we say it is.

We cannot have a pan-African account of history in which all Black and Brown people count as African in the secular account, but not the Christian one. Stated differently, if some secularists can look back to the greatness of our African past as the basis for Black identity now, then Black Christians can look to early African Christianity as their own. Therefore, it is historically inaccurate to say that *Africans* first heard of Christianity via slavery. The Christian story is ours too. It even stretches further back into early Christianity than

---

[2]Elizabeth Isichei, *A History of Christianity in Africa: From Antiquity to the Present* (London: SPCK, 1995), 17.

[3]Isichei, *A History of Christianity in Africa*, 17.

the three patriarchal sees of the emerging church catholic. Africans can be found at the beginning of the Jewish and later Christian story as recounted in the biblical text.

To press the point further, we turn our eyes from Egypt and move further south to the kingdom of Nubia in what we now call Sudan. We find that it was evangelized most successfully in the sixth century by the missionary Julian sent from Constantinople.[4] The speed at which Christianity became the official religion has led some to suggest that the Christian mission precedes the activities of Julian.[5] In any case, Nubia is an example of Christianity coming into Africa without any colonization.

Nubia is not the only kingdom that can claim a history of Christianity free of Western colonialism. Ethiopia has a similar story. It was evangelized by Frumentius in the fourth century. He was originally from Lebanon but received approval from Athanasius of Alexandria to evangelize Ethiopia.[6] This mission was the beginning of what became the Ethiopian Orthodox church, which still exists to this day.

These examples are not meant to diminish the damage done by the colonization of Africa by some Christians. That sin is part of our history. Nonetheless, we can see that people of African descent were persuaded of the beauty of the Christian message in its own right apart from colonization. Free Black people were able to read in the texts of the Old and New Testaments the story of a God who loved them and called them into his family. It is false to claim that modern Black Christians are in revolt against their heritage. If the Black community in our day is going to reclaim the lost bits of our

---

[4]Isichei, *A History of Christianity in Africa*, 30-31.
[5]Isichei, *A History of Christianity in Africa*, 30-31.
[6]Isichei, *A History of Christianity in Africa*, 32.

story, then let us recover the whole thing. The Black man or woman in America who goes back to Africa looking to find their roots will be surprised to find many Black and Brown ancestors staring them in the face proclaiming Christ is risen.

This chapter reflects on the significance of a select number of African figures in the Scriptures and their implications for Black faith today.

BLESSINGS FOR ALL: EPHRAIM, MANASSEH, AND A MULTIETHNIC ISRAEL

Most scholars of the book of Genesis make a distinction between the first eleven chapters and chapters twelve through fifty. The first eleven recount creation, the fall, the growth of human culture and the spread of sin. This spread of sin leads to a great act of uncreation, the flood. This divine judgment of the flood does not solve the problem of human sin. In the Genesis account, the people who leave the ark carry with them the same brokenness of their ancestors. This portion of redemptive history culminates in the tower of Babel, a human attempt to defy God's command to fill the earth with image bearers. Nonetheless, Genesis 11 ends with humanity scattered and God's purposes seemingly in peril.

God's response to human rebellion was to call Abram. His story marks a turning point in history. It is the start of the epic of Israel:

> Now the LORD said to Abram, "Go from your country and your kindred and your father's house to the land that I will show you. I will make of you a great nation, and I will bless you, and make your name great, so that you will be a blessing. I will bless those who bless you, and the one who curses you I will curse; and in you all the families of the earth shall be blessed." (Gen 12:1-3)

This promise to bless all the nations of the earth comes on the heels of the so-called table of nations outlined in Genesis 10:1-32. Thus, the nations to be blessed by Abraham are none other than the peoples outlined in those passages.[7] The link between the table of nations and the blessing of Abraham is important because the members of that list of nations would periodically be enemies of Israel during the twists and turns of her history. Nonetheless, the Abrahamic promises repeated in Genesis 13, 17, 22, 28, 35, and 48 show us that none of these enemies were intended to be enemies forever. God's eschatological vision is one of reconciliation. The Abrahamic promise of universal blessing serves as the theological fountainhead for the declarations that in the last days God would establish universal peace (Is 2:1-5).

This discussion of the Abrahamic blessing is relevant to Black identity because it shows that God's vision for his people was never limited to one ethnic group, culture, or nation. His plan was to bless the world *through* Abraham's descendants. Therefore, from the beginning God's vision included Black and Brown people. Insomuch as Christianity takes its bearing from the Old Testament, the global nature of Abraham's vision proves lie to any claim that the Messiah Jesus, the ultimate heir of Abraham (Mt 1:1; Gal 3:16), belongs only to Europe. God promised to make Abraham the father of many "nations," which includes the varied ethnic groups of the world.

Rather than seeing in the Genesis narrative an account of God's vision of a multiethnic people, many saw Genesis as the text inscribing blackness as cursed.[8] The pro-slavery faction in North America (and beyond) maintained that Black skin and enslavement were the result of the curse of Ham recounted in Genesis 9:20-27. No reasonable reading of Genesis could maintain (1) Canaan was the

---

[7]Victor P. Hamilton, *The Book of Genesis: Chapters 1–17*, NICOT (Grand Rapids, MI: Eerdmans, 1990), 374.

[8]David M. Goldenberg, "The Curse of Ham," in *The Curse of Ham: Race and Slavery in Early Judaism, Christianity, and Islam* (Princeton, NJ: Princeton University Press, 2003), 168-77.

ancestors of all Africans; (2) the curse was black skin; (3) the point of Genesis was to substantiate European dominance over African peoples. Nonetheless, the social location of the enslavers looking for justification for sin distorted the plain meaning of the text. The social location of African peoples who came to the text asking whether there was a place for us in this story gave them the eyes to see Genesis's true meaning.

The importance of Africans in fulfilling the Abrahamic promises can be seen in the much-neglected story of Jacob, Ephraim, and Manasseh. Black Christians will be familiar with the story of Joseph, who was enslaved and sold by his brothers to Egypt. Eventually Joseph rose in power, ending up second only to the Pharaoh (Gen 41:40). Pharaoh also gave Joseph an Egyptian wife, Asenath, by whom he had two sons, Ephraim and Manasseh.

After the dramatic reconciliation between Joseph and his brothers, the family is reunited and takes up residence in Egypt. Toward the end of Jacob's life, Joseph brings his two boys to be blessed by his father. Meeting these two half-Egyptian, half-Jewish boys causes Jacob to recall the promise that God made him many years prior:

> And Jacob said to Joseph, "God Almighty appeared to me at Luz in the land of Canaan, and he blessed me, and said to me, 'I am going to make you fruitful and increase your numbers; I will make of you a company of peoples, and will give this land to your offspring after you for a perpetual holding.' Therefore your two sons, who were born to you in the land of Egypt before I came to you in Egypt, are now mine; Ephraim and Manasseh shall be mine, just as Reuben and Simeon are." (Gen 48:3-5)

Jacob sees the *Brown flesh and African origin of these boys* as the beginning of God's fulfillment of his promise to make Jacob a community of different nations and ethnicities, and *for that reason he claims these two boys as his own.* These two boys become two of the twelve tribes of Israel. Egypt and Africa are not *outside* of God's people; African blood flows *into* Israel from the beginning as a fulfillment of the promise made to Abraham, Isaac, and Jacob.

As it relates to the twelve tribes, then, there was never a biologically "pure" Israel. Israel was always multiethnic and multinational. As a Black man, when I look to the biblical story, I do not see a story of someone else in which I find my place only by some feat of imagination. Instead God's purposes include me as an irreplaceable feature along with my African ancestors. We are the first of those joined to Abraham's family in anticipation of the rest of the nations of the earth.

Let us press our claim about blackness and the Bible a little further. One of the paradigmatic events in the life of Israel was the exodus event. Here God liberates the descendants of Abraham, Isaac, and Jacob from slavery. We have already seen that these Israelites were portrayed as having African blood.

What of those who left Egypt after a long period of slavery? Exodus 12:38 says that "a mixed crowd" went up with them. Who might this mixed crowd be? The phrase translated as "mixed crowd" usually refers to non-Israelites. In the other places that this phrase appears in the Old Testament, it refers to a number of different ethnic groups. That Moses has a large number of ethnic groups in mind is clear by his use of the word *many*. A better translation of Exodus 12:38 would be that a large number of different ethnic groups came out of Egypt. Given that we know that Cush (Nubia) had relations with Egypt it is not that big a stretch to believe that some of those who left Egypt were Black and that there were other Middle Eastern folks who departed with the Israelites.[9] This diverse gathering of Black and Brown bodies newly liberated from slavery is

---

[9]Douglas K. Stuart, *Exodus*, NAC (Nashville: Broadman & Holman, 2006), 303-4.

directly connected to God's promise to Abraham that he would make him the father of many nations.

We need to be as clear as possible about this. When it comes to the question of Black presence in the Bible, it is not a question of finding our place in someone else's story. The Bible is first and foremost the story of God's desire to create a people. We are encompassed within that desire.

DAVID'S SON: THE IDEAL KING AND THE NATIONS OF THE WORLD

There is a strong link between Abraham and ethnic diversity because God promised to use Abraham to bless the nations and peoples of the earth. Given the strong link between the story of Abraham and ethnic diversity, the link between the Abrahamic promises and the Davidic promises take on special significance.[10] Psalm 72 presents itself as one of the final prayers ever written by David. It concludes with "the prayers of David, son of Jesse are ended" (Ps 72:20, my translation). There is something climactic about this text that captures something essential about Davidic hope. Within the text, the prayer is centered around Solomon and his impending rule. What hope does David have for his son and how are these hopes connected to the hopes of the Black and brown Bodies and souls that look for comfort in these texts?

David makes the following request:

Give the king your justice, O God,
    and your righteousness to a king's son.
May he judge your people with righteousness,
    and your poor with justice.
May the mountains yield prosperity for the people,
    and the hills, in righteousness.

---

[10]On the link between the promise God made to David in 2 Samuel 7:14 and Genesis 12:1-3, see Craig E. Morrison, *2 Samuel*, Berit Olam (Collegeville, MN: Liturgical Press, 2013), 100.

> May he defend the cause of the poor of the people,
>
> > give deliverance to the needy,
> >
> > and crush the oppressor. (Ps 72:1-4)

This prayer is not just speaking a word about a child, but as words to the future king, it presents a vision for the future *government* of Israel. He prays that the *government* might be a place where justice flourishes, and the afflicted can turn to the most powerful person in the country for deliverance.

This is not just good news for Israel. It is good news for the whole world. Psalm 72:8 continues, "May he rule from sea to sea / and from the River to the ends of the earth" (NIV). This is an expansion of the promise God made to Abraham in Genesis 15:17-18, which reads,

> When the sun had gone down and it was dark, a smoking fire pot and a flaming torch passed between these pieces. On that day the LORD made a covenant with Abram, saying, "To your descendants I give this land, from the river of Egypt to the great river, the river Euphrates."

According to the psalmist, the promised offspring of Abraham is not simply entitled to the land of Israel, but the entire earth. The promises to Abraham, then, are fulfilled throughout the worldwide rule of the promised son of David. This is not a mere expansion of territory. It is an expansion of justice and concern for the afflicted (Ps 72:1-4) as a fulfillment of the Abrahamic promises.[11]

We know that the Abrahamic promises inform his vision for his son because he evokes them later in the psalm when he says, "All nations will be blessed through him, and they will call him blessed."

---

[11]On the importance of Psalm 72 and the link between the Abrahamic and Davidic promises in Paul, see Esau McCaulley, *Sharing in the Son's Inheritance* (London: T&T Clark, 2019), 146-59.

This is almost a direct quotation of Genesis 12:3 refocused around the son of David.[12]

What do Abraham and David together mean for the Black and Brown bodies spread throughout the globe? It means that the vision of Hebrew Scriptures is one in which the worldwide rule of the Davidic king brings longed-for justice and righteousness to all people groups.

Given the fact that the future Davidic kingdom is depicted as just and multiethnic, it is important to remember the emphasis on Jesus' Davidic and Abrahamic sonship throughout the New Testament:

> An account of the genealogy of Jesus the Messiah, the *son of David*, the *son of Abraham*. (Mt 1:1)

> When he heard that it was Jesus of Nazareth, he began to shout out and say, "Jesus, *Son of David*, have mercy on me!" (Mk 10:47)

> Your ancestor *Abraham rejoiced that he would see my day*; he saw it and was glad. (Jn 8:56)

> For I tell you that Christ has become a servant of the circumcised on behalf of the truth of God in order that he might confirm the promises given to the patriarchs. . . .
> And again Isaiah says,
> "*The root of Jesse* shall come,
>   the one who rises to rule the Gentiles;
>   in him the Gentiles shall hope." (Rom 15:8, 12, emphasis added)

> Then one of the elders said to me, "Do not weep. See, the Lion of the tribe of Judah, *the Root of David*, has conquered, so that he can open the scroll and its seven seals." (Rev 5:5, emphasis added)

These texts all claim that the promises held long in abeyance are now reaching their fulfillment in Jesus. Scholars may respond and say

---

[12]McCaulley, *Inheritance*, 114.

that there were not clear expectations for the Son of David that all Jews everywhere expected to be fulfilled.[13] That is fair enough, but the early Christians seemed to agree that the Old Testament contained a vision for the conversion of the nations of the earth in the promises made to David and Abraham. They saw in Jesus and the mission that he gave to his followers the fulfillment of those promises. According to these Christians, Jesus is the manifestation of God's love for the ethnicities of the world. Texts such as Psalm 72 claim that when the Son of David takes the throne his rule will be marked by justice for all those nations under his dominion. The New Testament writers were convinced that his rule began with the resurrection of Jesus from the dead and that God had called them to announce this good news of Jesus' kingship to the world. It seems from the perspective of the New Testament writers that all the ethnic groups of the world are necessary for the story to reach its proper end.

John's word to his congregation—"We declare to you what we have seen and heard so that you also may have fellowship with us; and truly our fellowship is with the Father and with his Son Jesus Christ. We are writing these things so that our joy may be complete" (1 Jn 1:3-4)—could be rewritten to say that the joyous fellowship of the people of God is incomplete without the ethnic groups he promised to include in his family. God's vision for his people is not for the elimination of ethnicity to form a colorblind uniformity of sanctified blandness. Instead God sees the creation of a community of different cultures united by faith in his Son as a manifestation of the expansive nature of his grace. This expansiveness is unfulfilled unless the differences are seen and celebrated, not as ends unto

---

[13]See Esau McCaulley, *Inheritance*, 1-2, 28-46, for a review of the state of the question on Paul and messianism, which is indicative of the denials of messianic expectation throughout the New Testament.

themselves, but as particular manifestations of the power of the Spirit to bring forth the same holiness among different peoples and cultures for the glory of God.

TWO AFRICANS, ONE CROSS: BLACK PRESENCE AT THE BEGINNING OF CHRISTIANITY

The Hebrew Scriptures look to a multiethnic fellowship within the people of God. Was this vision and the inclusion of Black and Brown bodies ever realized in the New Testament? Were the promises to the patriarchs and the vision of the kingdom lost when the first worshipers of Jesus finally gathered to sing praises to his name? To answer that question, let us begin before the resurrection with the last moments of the life of Christ.

It has often been said that Mary was the first disciple because her yes to God (Lk 1:38) led to the birth of Christ. Paul likened his ministry to labor pains (Gal 4:19), but Mary experienced real, physical pain to bring the Messiah into the world. For that she receives perpetual honor and will ever be known as the blessed one.

Nonetheless, the picture of discipleship that comes to define early Christianity is the image of taking up one's cross (Mt 10:38; 16:24). Paul expresses a similar idea in Romans when he says, "If children, then heirs, heirs of God and joint heirs with Christ—if, in fact, we *suffer* with him so that we may also be *glorified* with him" (Rom 8:17). In the strange economy of the kingdom, the cross is glory. But who then is the first bearer of the cross other than our Lord?

Mark adds an interesting detail in his account of the passion of Christ. He says that Simon of Cyrene was compelled to carry the cross.[14] Cyrene is a city in North Africa in what we now call Libya. In the same

---

[14]There is some debate as to whether this should be seen as an act of discipleship. See Luke Powery, "Gospel of Mark," in *True to Our Native Land: An African American New Testament Commentary* (Minneapolis, MN: Fortress Press, 2007), 150.

way that Mary's giving birth is seen an image of Christian faithfulness, Simon's cross carrying is a physical manifestation of the spiritual reality that Christian discipleship involves the embrace of suffering.

Mark states that Simon is the father of Rufus and Alexander. Why mention these men? The most logical answer is that Rufus and Alexander were known to Mark's audience.[15] If anyone was tempted to doubt the veracity of Mark's account of the crucifixion, they could ask Rufus and Alexander, living members of the Christian community. We cannot say for sure when or how, but at some point this African father became convinced of the truth of the gospel and passed that faith to his sons and possibly his wife (Rom 16:13).[16] At the moment in which Christ is reconciling the world to himself on the cross, an African family is making its first steps toward the kingdom.

The family of Simon the Cyrene are not the only African believers in the early church. The book of Acts tells us that the persecution of Christians in the aftermath of Stephen's martyrdom led some believers to leave Jerusalem. Those fleeing began to preach the gospel outside the holy city (Acts 8:4). This evangelistic work fulfilled the promise that believers would be witnesses to Jesus from Jerusalem to the ends of the earth (Acts 1:8).

Philip was one of those who left Jerusalem and spread the gospel. Acts 8:26 tells us that as he went along an angel directed him to take the road from Jerusalem to Gaza. The angel redirected him so that he might encounter an Ethiopian eunuch in charge of the treasury for the queen mother of Ethiopia.[17] Within the narrative world of

---

[15]Powery, "Gospel of Mark," 150; see also Richard Bauckham, *Jesus and the Eyewitnesses: The Gospels as Eyewitness Testimony* (Grand Rapids, MI: Eerdmans, 2006), 51.

[16]Bauckham, *Jesus and the Eyewitnesses*, 52n49.

[17]J. F. Prewitt, "Candace," in *International Standard Bible Encyclopedia (Revised)*, ed. Geoffery W. Bromiley, Accordance electronic edition, version 1.2 (Grand Rapids, MI: Eerdmans, 1979), 591.

Acts, the conversion of this Ethiopian manifests God's concern for the nations of the world.

Philip approaches him and discovers that he is reading a passage from Isaiah. The Ethiopian could only be familiar with Isaiah if he already knew something of the God of Israel. This shows a deep African connection to the God of the Bible. The passage that he was reading from Isaiah says:

> Like a sheep he was led to the slaughter,
> > and like a lamb silent before its shearer,
> > so he does not open his mouth.
> In his humiliation justice was denied him.
> > Who can describe his generation?
> > For his life is taken away from the earth.
> > (Acts 8:32-33; Is 53:7-8 LXX)

This text is an enigma to the Ethiopian, so he asks Philip to explain it. We are not told what Philip says. We do know that Isaiah 52:13–53:12, which recounts the fate of the suffering servant, was a central text in early Christian interpretation of Jesus' death (Gal 1:4; 2:20; Rom 4:25; 8:32). In its Old Testament context, the servant narrative of Isaiah 53 is preceded by the announcement of a new exodus:

> Depart, depart, go out from there!
> > Touch no unclean thing;
> go out from the midst of it, purify yourselves,
> > you who carry the vessels of the Lord.
> For you shall not go out in haste,
> > and you shall not go in flight;
> for the Lord will go before you,
> > and the God of Israel will be your rear guard. (Is 52:11-12)

But the question remains, How can this liberation that Isaiah foresees occur? The answer is the servant of Isaiah 53. He is the one who was "despised and rejected" but nonetheless "bore our suffering" and was "pierced for our transgressions." The early Christians interpreted Isaiah 53 as a reference to Jesus whose death for sins reconciles Israel and the world to God. This might have been what Philip explained to the Ethiopian. The person described in this passage, the one who suffers to reconcile us, is none other than Jesus the Messiah who is alive and reigning with God on high. In other words, Philip told him about the glorious contradiction of a crucified Messiah, and the gospel did its work.

When we combine the account of Simon with that of the Ethiopian eunuch we find that *two Africans* are brought to the Christian faith by means of powerful encounters with the cross. This story of Jesus crucified and risen drew the Ethiopian in and led him to be baptized. Again, this shows clearly that Africans are drawn to Christianity in much the same way as everyone else. Christ died for our sins to reconcile us to God.

I find significance in the fact that the Ethiopian eunuch was reading from a particular portion of the servant's narrative, namely the portion where it says that justice was denied him.[18] The eunuch was not materially poor, but as one who had been castrated he was in a socially ambiguous position because eunuchs were often despised.[19] In a culture with strictly defined gender roles, he would be seen as aberrant. Is it possible that he felt that what had been done to him was a grave injustice—for which he was forced, for his own safety, to keep silent like the silently suffering Christ? Was there a point of connection between the rejection the servant experienced and the rejection that the eunuch experienced? If the eunuch did

---

[18]J. Alec Motyer, *The Prophecy of Isaiah: An Introduction and Commentary* (Downers Grove, IL: InterVarsity Press, 1993), 435, thinks that the text highlights that failure to follow proper legal procedure. It was a sham trial.

[19]Michael C. Parson, *Acts*, Paideia (Grand Rapids, MI: Baker, 2008), 120.

connect with Jesus as the one who suffered injustice, then he would be the starting point of an unending stream of Black believers who found their own dignity and self-worth through the dignity and power that Christ received at his resurrection. Maybe the eunuch's conversion is an example of the inversion spoken of by Paul:

> Consider your own call, brothers and sisters: not many of you were wise by human standards, not many were powerful, not many were of noble birth. But God chose what is foolish in the world to shame the wise; God chose what is weak in the world to shame the strong; God chose what is low and despised in the world, things that are not, to reduce to nothing things that are, so that no one might boast in the presence of God. (1 Cor 1:26-29)

This eunuch as a "despised thing" found hope in the shamed Messiah whose resurrection lifts those with imposed indignities to places of honor. This indignity was not ontological. The eunuch remained an image bearer. Christ showed the eunuch who he truly was. Christ, similarly, does not convey worth on ontologically inferior blackness. Those of African descent are image bearers in the same way as anyone else. What Christ does is liberate us to become what we are truly meant to be, redeemed and transformed citizens of the kingdom.

These reflections on suffering injustice and indignity as a point of connection do not stand in competition with the atoning work of Christ on the cross. It does highlight a particular aspect of Black theological reflection to be considered more fully in the next chapter, namely that through the cross Black Christians recover their sense of self. We take comfort in the fact that the Son suffered injustice but was nonetheless vindicated by God. This gives us hope for our own vindication.

What do the stories of Simon and the Ethiopian eunuch mean for Black Christianity? They show that the story of early Christianity is in part our story. We are at the cross. We are at the beginning of the emerging Christian community.[20] There is no evidence that Simon or the Ethiopian felt that one couldn't be African and Christian. Their stories also demonstrate that the cross played a strong role in their conversion and that a connection to Jesus' unjust suffering may stand as a crucial aspect of early African faith. Finally, we see in the story of Simon the possibility that the faith that began with his encounter with the cross was passed down organically to his family members who were well known among the first readers of Mark's gospel.

THE WAY THE STORY ENDS: JOHN'S VISION

I have argued that those of African descent have been a part of God's people from the beginning. We see this in the inclusion of Africans within the nation of Israel and in the conversion of Africans at the start of Christianity. We must not lose sight of the fact that the story of Christianity ultimately belongs to the triune God who glories in bringing the nations of the world into his family. Nonetheless, the conversion of those of African descent is one manifestation of his will to gather a people. To close out this reflection on the Bible and Black identity, I want to explore the relationship between conversion and our ethnic identity by means of the book of Revelation.

It has become common to claim that strong affirmations of ethnic identity are improper for Christians. Some white Christians have even begun to claim that they do not see color. This is rooted in a strange appropriation of Martin Luther King Jr.'s "I Have a Dream" speech. In that message King speaks of his vision of Black kids and white kids playing together and people being judged, not by "the color of their skin," but the "content of their character."[21] King's point

---

[20]See also the African leadership noted in Acts 13:1-3.

[21]Martin Luther King Jr., "I Have a Dream" in *I Have a Dream: Speeches and Writings that Changed the World*, ed. James M. Washington (New York: HarperCollins, 1992), 101-6.

was never that ethnicity and culture are irrelevant, but that they should not be the cause of discrimination. King often called on African Americans to take pride in their culture and heritage:

> The Negro will only be free when he reaches down to the inner depths of his own being and signs with the pen and ink of assertive manhood his own emancipation proclamation. . . . The Negro must boldly throw off the manacles of self-abnegation and say to himself and to the world, "I am somebody. I am a person. I am a man with dignity and honor. I have a rich and noble history, however painful and exploited that history has been. Yes, I was a slave through my foreparents, and I'm not ashamed of that. I'm ashamed of the people who were so sinful to make me a slave." Yes, we must stand up and say, "I'm black, but I'm black and beautiful." This, this self-affirmation is the black man's need, made compelling by the white man's crimes against him.[22]

Far from being colorblind, King called on his people to look upon themselves as Black and see in that blackness something beautiful. In doing so King echoes the vision of Revelation in which each ethnicity brings its own unique glory to God.

Others argue for this colorblind vision based on a misunderstanding of Galatians 3:28 in which Paul says, "There is no Jew nor Greek, no male and female, there is no slave and free, for you are all one in Christ" (my translation). Some take this passage to mean that Paul claims our identity in Christ cancels out our ethnic identities. But this is strange for many reasons. Few would claim that they do not see gender because of our identity in Christ. In addition, Paul makes much of two aspects of his mission work that call into question his lack of racial (or more properly speaking ethnic) consciousness:

---

[22]Martin Luther King Jr., "Where Do We Go from Here?" in I Have a Dream: Speeches and Writings that Changed the World, ed. James M. Washington (New York: HarperCollins, 1992), 169-79.

(1) he calls himself apostle to the *Gentiles* (Rom 11:13), and (2) he speaks of his missional flexibility as it relates to Jew and Gentile culture for the sake of effective evangelism (1 Cor 9:20-23).[23] How could Paul make a point of evangelizing Gentiles if he didn't care about ethnicity? How could he speak about different mission strategies unless he recognized the differences between Jews and Gentiles? The colorblind interpretation of Paul cuts against the grain of his entire ministry.

The colorblind reading of Galatians 3:28 is most flawed because it doesn't take the context of the book of Galatians seriously enough. The question that runs from one end of Galatians to the other is, Who are the rightful heirs to the promises made to Abraham? Paul's opponents claim that one must believe in Christ and do the works of the law to become an heir while Paul claims that faith makes one an heir to the inheritance. Paul's denial of class, gender, and ethnicity must be read in light of this fundamental question. Paul's point is that being a Jew does not make you more of an heir to the promises in Christ than being a Gentile. It is a question about standing as it relates to the inheritance, not ethnic identity full stop.[24]

Even if Paul cannot be coopted to negate ethnic identity in Christianity, some might say that we lack a *positive account* of what it means to be African, Latino/a, or Asian in Christ. John's words in Revelation provide the key to understanding the role that our ethnic identities play in our Christian lives.

John's apocalypse begins with a vision of the risen and reigning Lord that leaves John undone (Rev 1:1-20). His epistle then transitions to a series of letters to the seven churches (Rev 2:1–3:22) and

---

[23]Anthony C. Thiselton, *The First Epistle to the Corinthians: A Commentary on the Greek Text*, NIGTC (Grand Rapids, MI: Eerdmans, 2000), 702.

[24]For a fuller discussion of Galatians 3:28, see McCaulley, *Sharing in the Son's Inheritance*, 159-69.

an image of praise in heaven (Rev 4:1-11). Later, John will reveal a vision of the future that includes both judgment and salvation (Rev 6–8), but there is a problem.

According to John, there was no one in heaven or earth worthy to open the scrolls that contain God's will for the future (Rev 5:1-4). John articulates the central question of human history. What is our future and who controls it? What will become of us? No human agent is worthy. The politicians of Jesus' day and ours, regardless of their pretentions to power, are not in control.

There is only one person sufficient to unfurl human history and bring about God's purposes, the one who gave himself for our salvation in weakness and now reigns in power. Revelation 5:5 says, "Then one of the elders said to me, 'Do not weep. See, the Lion of the tribe of Judah, the Root of David, has conquered, so that he can open the scroll and its seven seals.'" Jesus as the risen and reigning king has won for himself the ability to order history. This is relevant to the question of *ethnic identity* because Jesus' vision for the climax of human history lauds the importance of ethnicity.

Revelation 7:9-10 looks to the end, and at the end we encounter ethnic diversity:

> After this I looked, and there was a great multitude that no one could count, from every nation, from all tribes and peoples and languages, standing before the throne and before the Lamb, robed in white, with palm branches in their hands. They cried out in a loud voice, saying,
>
> "Salvation belongs to our God who is seated on the throne, and to the Lamb!"

The reference to the *multitude* calls to mind the promises made to Abraham that he would become the father of many nations. It also evokes the promises made to David that his son would gather and bless the nations of the world by his gracious rule. John mentions four aspects of this multitude. It includes people from every nation, tribe, people, and language. Each in its own way highlights diversity. These distinct peoples, cultures, and languages are *eschatological, everlasting*. At the end, we do not find the elimination of difference. Instead the very diversity of cultures is a manifestation of God's glory.

God's eschatological vision for the reconciliation of all things in his Son requires my blackness and my neighbor's Latina identity to endure forever. Colorblindness is sub-biblical and falls short of the glory of God.[25] What is it that unites this diversity? It is not cultural assimilation, but the fact that we worship the Lamb. This means that the gifts that our cultures have are not ends in themselves. Our distinctive cultures represent the means by which we give honor to God. He is honored through the diversity of tongues singing the same song. Therefore inasmuch as I modulate my blackness or neglect my culture, I am placing limits on the gifts that God has given me to offer to his church and kingdom. The vision of the kingdom is incomplete without Black and Brown persons worshiping alongside white persons as part of one kingdom under the rule of one king.

CONCLUSION

This chapter explored the relationship between Black identity and the Bible. There are two groups that want to separate us from the Christian story. One group claims that Christianity is fundamentally a white religion. This is simply historically false. The center of early Christianity was in the Middle East and North Africa. But deeper than the historical question is the biblical one. Who owns the Christian story as it is recorded in the texts that make up the canon? I have contended that Christianity is ultimately a story about God

---

[25]This does not mean that God offers an unqualified yes to every aspect of our cultures. Individually and corporately all things must be transformed to embody fully God's purposes.

and his purposes. That is good news. God has always intended to gather a diverse group of people to worship him. The energy of the biblical story after the fall finds its footing in the promises made to Abraham that he would be the father of many nations. In the stories of Ephraim and Manasseh, we see that this promise was first fulfilled by bringing two African boys into the people of God. We saw the inclusion of Africans again reiterated when a multiethnic group of people left Egypt. These promises to Abraham were expanded into a kingdom vision through the hopes of a Davidic king who would rule and bless the nations. The repeated claim of the New Testament is that Jesus is this king who brings these promises to fulfillment. He gathers the nations under him. We see this vision become flesh throughout the conversion of Africans: Simon and his family as well as the Ethiopian eunuch. Just as at the origin of the Israelites, at the origin of the church we find Black and Brown believers. Finally, we argued that at the end, when we finally meet our savior, we do not come to him as a faceless horde but as transformed believers from every tribe, tongue, and nation. When the Black Christian enters the community of faith, she is not entering a strange land. She is finding her way home.

SIX

WHAT SHALL WE DO WITH THIS RAGE?

THE BIBLE AND BLACK ANGER

■ ■ ■

*To be a Negro in this country and to be relatively
conscious is to be in a rage almost all the time.*
JAMES BALDWIN

*For the message of the cross is foolishness to those who are
perishing, but to us who are being saved it is the power of God.*
1 CORINTHIANS 1:18 NIV

I WAS EIGHT YEARS OLD the first time someone called me a nigger.
It all began around midmorning when I started to feel sick at
Rolling Hills Elementary School. I was not a kid prone to escape
the classroom. My mother worked during the day, and there was
no one to take care of me if I fell ill. On this particular day I was in
bad enough shape to call my mother at her factory job at Chrysler.
I dutifully went to the school office, where they dialed the number

that was on the emergency contact card and handed me the phone. I asked to speak to Laurie McCaulley, but the speaker said that I had the wrong number and abruptly hung up the phone. I told the office manager to try again in case she dialed the wrong number. Again she dialed the number and gave me the phone. Again, I nervously asked for Laurie McCaulley. The man on the other line angrily said something along the lines of "I told you that you have the wrong number. . . . Can't you niggers even use the phone?" before again hanging up.

I was aware of my blackness before that phone call. But prior to that conversation, my blackness was wrapped up in the soothing warmth of normalcy. My church was Black; my school was Black, and my sports teams were Black. When we cleaned our home, Black soul music shouting that "I am Black and I am proud" played in the background. At the time, I had no idea that James Brown was sounding a note of protest against the dehumanization of Black persons. His defiance went unheard. On the phone that morning, I experienced my blackness as the object of derision. I remember wondering how he could tell that I was Black without seeing me. Was it my diction or the register of my voice? Did my blackness seep through the phone and offend his sensibilities? I also recall the rage building alongside my awareness of my powerlessness. I had been emotionally assaulted, but there was no way to respond. I was helpless before this white man who didn't know me. The sickness that led me to the office that day morphed into a sense of dread. I think that I knew that this was the beginning, not the end of my indignities.[1]

---

[1]Speaking of his own encounter with blackness as danger, W. E. B. Du Bois said, "It is in the early days of rollicking boyhood that the revelation first bursts upon one, all in a day, as it were. I remember well when *the shadow swept across me*." W. E. B. Du Bois, *The Souls of Black Folk* (New York: Dover Publications, 1903, 1994), 1-2, emphasis added.

A LITANY OF BLACK SUFFERING

Little Black girls and Black boys collect these slights, large and small, as they navigate the cities and towns, the highways and backroads of these United States. Little boys see their blackness shift from cuteness to danger. Women find themselves pushed and pulled into sexual stereotypes that present them as objects of pleasure. As hips and thighs develop so do the threats to their safety. Black children are taught strategies of survival that often come at the cost of their childhood or basic humanity. There is a sense of not-rightness that grows in young Black hearts.

We glean our limitations by contrast with the carefreeness of our white counterparts. The anger grows, and we often have no place to put it, so we turn to the closest thing at hand. We harm each other and set ridiculous standards of respect. We violently demand the respect of our Black friends and neighbors because we are hounded by disrespect in white spaces. I lived in fear of breaking one of these "neighborhood rules" and becoming an outlet for pent-up Black frustration. I grew up around Black men who hit Black women and I was helpless to stop it. The rage grew. I was mad at white people. I was mad at my own people. I was infuriated by my own helplessness. This rage is a part of the lived experience of many African Americans who are, in the words of James Baldwin, "relatively conscious."

Many African Americans who abandoned Christianity were in part motivated by this rage. Granting that Christianity is not a white man's religion, it is nonetheless true that white Christians have and continue to hurt us. I have argued that the Bible shows that as far back as we can go in the biblical story we will find African brothers and sisters participating in God's great redemptive work. It is also true that a recourse to history will show that as far back into America's story as we want to go we will see the heavy boot of white supremacy stepping on the backs of Black women and men.

Black bodies enter the laws of this land, not as persons but as an accounting tool to determine the voting rights of white men (the Three-Fifths Compromise). Before that we were mercilessly dragged from our native land and flung to the far ends of the world to be beaten, bred, raped, and degraded. Families were ripped apart and all the doors of opportunity were closed to us. We were despised and rejected by men, seen as cursed and abandoned by God. We were those from whom men hid their faces.[2]

The year 1865 did not signal freedom, but simply the beginning of a different type of struggle. The years of reconstruction saw some expansion of Black opportunity. However Black bodies were again sacrificed at the altar of compromise in 1877 when, in exchange for the presidency, Republicans agreed to remove troops from the south. What followed was a series of ever-increasing Jim Crow laws that robbed Black people of dignity and opportunity.

And what more shall we say? For the time would fail me to tell of the lynching tree, the Red summer, the dogs and the water hoses, the sit-ins, Emmett Till, Medgar Evers, Martin Luther King Jr., the people who defied governors and presidents, braved mobs, and sang victory, people of whom the world was not worthy. The history of Black people in this country is a litany of suffering. Yet we are definitely more than this suffering. There is a thread of victory woven into the tale of despair. We are still here! Still, sometimes it's hard to see that thread when the cloth is stained with blood.

---

[2]On the likeness of the slave auction to the passion, see William James Jennings, *The Christian Imagination: Theology and the Origins of Race* (New Haven, CT: Yale University Press, 2010), 19-24.

When a Black person learns the history of our suffering and then continues to experience the aftershocks of the seismic disruption of slavery in our ongoing oppression, a feeling of rage or even nihilism begins to rise. Our suffering is not an inadvertent consequence of an otherwise just system. It was designed to be that way. What are we do with this anger, this pain? How does Christianity speak to it? What does the cross have to say, not simply to human suffering, but the particular suffering of African Americans?

I want to present four Christian reflections on the issue of Black anger and suffering. First, I argue that Israel's pain and anger as recorded in the prophets and the psalter provide a means of processing Black grief. Secondly, I contend that the prophets warn that the ever-spiraling cycle of violence is a dead end. Turning to the New Testament, I maintain that the cross functions as the *end of the cycle of vengeance and death* and that the cross is a place where God enters into our pain. Finally, I suggest that the central biblical themes of the resurrection, ascension, and the final judgment are necessary in any account of Black anger and pain.

BY THE RIVERS OF BABYLON: ISRAEL'S
PERSONAL AND CORPORATE RAGE

African Americans are not very far from Israel in carrying within our history a long list of enemies and injustices, personal and corporate. The tale of this suffering can be found in Israel's psalms of lament, especially its imprecatory psalms.[3] Some have claimed that because of the harsh calls for vengeance in the imprecatory psalms that they are "impossible to use in Christian worship."[4] These psalms are seen as impossible to use because when speaking of

---

[3]On lament and imprecatory psalms, see Bernhard W. Anderson, *Out of the Depths: The Psalms Speak for Us Today* (Louisville, KY: Westminster John Knox Press, 2000), 49-76.
[4]Anderson, *Out of the Depths*, 70.

their enemies their authors ask God to allow "their eyes be darkened so they cannot see, / and their backs be bent forever. / Pour out your wrath on them; / let your fierce anger overtake them" (Ps 69:23-24).

Within the psalms, we find more than a mere call for the darkening of eyes and bending of backs. The psalms call for the complete economic and social collapse of their enemies resulting in death. Psalm 109 says,

> When he is tried, let him be found guilty;
>> let his prayer be counted as sin.
> May his days be few;
>> may another seize his position.
> May his children be orphans,
>> and his wife a widow.
> May his children wander about and beg;
>> may they be driven out of the ruins they inhabit. (Ps 109:7-10)

These are the words of a people who know *rage*, a people who know what it is like to turn to those with power hoping for recompense only to be pushed further into the mud. These are the words of those who walk past homes and families living in luxury knowing that this wealth is bought with the price of their suffering. The oppressor's children live at ease while children of the oppressed starve. The rich man's wife has the latest fashions while the oppressed man's wife remains in rags. We will address God's response to these psalms shortly, but first we must listen to the injustices that give rise to the anger. It is an anger born of powerlessness; it is a cry to the only one who is left to right these wrongs, God. To whom could the battered and bruised of Israel turn if not God?

Possibly the most difficult of these psalms of vengeance is Psalm 137. The achingly beautiful longing that opens the psalm is only matched by the startlingly violent end. Psalm 137 is written from the perspective of Israelites who experienced the trauma of the destruction of the temple, the burning of Jerusalem, and the rape and murder that accompany modern and ancient conquests of the city.[5] These are the words of survivors who look back on the devastation of what once was Israel and could only mourn. The King James version captures it best: "By the rivers of Babylon, there we sat down, yea, we wept, when we remembered Zion. We hanged our harps upon the willows in the midst thereof" (Ps 137:1-2 KJV).

No one who has read of Black families being ripped apart after having survived the middle passage will fail to see the deep kinship with Israel in our shared stories of trauma. Gomez Azurara recounts the scene of enslaved Africans arriving at Lagos, Portugal, in 1844:

> But to increase their sufferings still more, there now arrived those who had the charge of division of the captives . . . it was needful to part fathers from sons, husbands from wives, brothers from brothers . . . and who could finish that partition without great toil. For as often as they had placed them in one part the sons, seeing their fathers in another, rose with great energy and rushed over to them; the mothers clasped their other children in their arms, and threw themselves flat on the ground with them; receiving blows with little pity for their own flesh, if only they might not be torn from them.[6]

We do not have the record of the psalms composed by these Black mothers and fathers, sons and daughters, but we do have the psalms of the survivors of Israel.

---

[5] Frank-Lothar Hossfeld and Erich Zenger, *Psalms 3: A Commentary on Psalms 101–150*, ed. Klaus Baltzer, trans. Linda M. Maloney, Hermeneia 19c (Minneapolis, MN: Fortress Press, 2011), 513.

[6] Gomes Eanes de Azurara, *The Chronicle of the Discovery and Conquest of Guinea*, 2 vols. (London: Hakluyt Society, 1896–99), 80-81, as quoted in Willie James Jennings, *The Christian Imagination: Theology and the Origins of Race* (New Haven, CT: Yale, 2010), 27.

These survivors, still reeling from the events that forever changed their lives, received a demand from their captors. The Babylonians wanted to hear some songs of Jerusalem (Ps 137:3-5). They wanted Israel to forget their anger and provide mirth for their captors. Here we encounter the psychological warfare that attaches itself to physical warfare. Not only did their captors take their land, their property, and their very bodies, now they demanded their emotions as well. They did not want to see the impact of their crimes on the faces of Israelites. They wanted the Israelites to accept their place joyfully.

Here again we are reminded of all the ways, large and small, that Black bodies and emotions were managed. This was captured most powerfully in Paul Laurence Dunbar's "We Wear the Mask":

> We wear the mask that grins and lies,
> It hides our cheeks and shades our eyes,—
> This debt we pay to human guile;
> With torn and bleeding hearts we smile.[7]

The dancing and jolly negro as one content with his place as servant was and remains a trope in fiction, advertisements, and film.

On this occasion Israel refused the mask; they had reached the edge of their submission. There was a piece of themselves that even in defeat they refused to relinquish. This refusal, embedded in the traditions of Israel, gives space for Black resistance. We can refuse to sing. Psalm 137 reminds us that it is possible and even required for our own survival to say that we will not sing and dance for our masters. Instead we will remember what was done to us. It is the duty of survivors to remember.

Psalm 137 is more than a personal memory of an oppressed people. It is a call for God to remember. It speaks of a reckoning:

---

[7]Paul Laurence Dunbar, "We Wear the Mask," *Lyrics of Lowly Life* (New York: Dodd, Mead, and Company, 1896), 167.

> Remember, O LORD, the children of Edom in the day of Jerusalem;
> who said, Rase it, rase it, even to the foundation thereof.
>
> O daughter of Babylon, who art to be destroyed; happy shall he be,
> that rewardeth thee as thou hast served us.
>
> Happy shall he be, that taketh and dasheth thy little ones against
> the stones. (Ps 137:7-9 KJV)

There are two groups remembered here. Those who oppressed Israel (the Babylonians) and those who rejoiced in Israel's downfall (the Edomites). But what kind of person of faith could ask that babies' heads be dashed by rocks, and in what sense can we receive these texts as in a meaningful sense Christian? In response I ask, what kind of prayer would you expect Israel to pray after watching the murder of their children and the destruction of their families? What kinds of words of vengeance lingered in the hearts of the Black slave women and men when they found themselves at the mercy of their enslavers' passions?

Psalm 137 is not merely a shout of defiance. It is a prayer addressed to God. Traumatized communities must be able to tell God the truth about what they feel. We must trust that God can handle those emotions. God can listen to our cries for vengeance, and as the one sovereign over history he gets to choose how to respond. Psalm 137 does not take power from God and give it to us. It is an affirmation of his power in the midst of deep pain and estrangement.

The fact that Psalm 137 became a part of the biblical canon means that the suffering of the traumatized is a part of the permanent record. God wanted Israel and us to know what human sin had done to the powerless. By recording this in Israel's sacred texts, God made their problems our problems. Psalm 137 calls on the gathered community to make sure that this type of trauma is never repeated.

What theological resources does Psalm 137 give to Black rage and pain? It gives us permission to remember and feel. It allows us to bring the depth of our experiences to God. Psalm 137 makes the suf-fering of the traumatized a corporate reality that moves with us through history.[8]

Based on the example of Psalm 137, I contend that Black Chris-tians can and must articulate what has happened to us to God and to others as a part of the healing process. We must tell the truth. Like the later Israelite readers of Psalm 137, the pain of the Black past must be carried forward and remembered as a testimony to what sin can and will do to the helpless. The beginning of the answer to Black anger is the knowledge that God hears and sees our pain. This means that an elementary school kid first introduced to racial trauma is at least equipped with a place to put his pain. They are borne up to heaven in prayer. More than that, their pain is not theirs to bear alone; it is wrapped up in the wider community's hope for justice. Can we say more?

A LARGER VISION: TOWARD A SOLUTION TO ISRAEL'S RAGE

If we end our discussion of Israel's rage and Black rage with simply a call for God to act, we are not being true to the fullness of the biblical witness. Sometimes we need to lament injustice and call for God to right wrongs. This is good and fair, but God's word to us is more than "vengeance is mine saith the Lord." The miracle of Israel's Scriptures is not that there are calls to repay our enemies to the full. That is the stuff of human existence. The miracle of Israel's witness is that the Old Testament could imagine something *beyond blood vengeance.*

I have in mind biblical prophets whose writings addressed those in exile. These were the descendants of those who had experienced the traumatic removal from their homes and the destruction of

---

[8]I am not the first to link Black suffering and Psalm 137. See Frederick Douglass, "What to a Slave Is the Fourth of July," speech, July 5, 1852, Rochester, New York, http://mass humanities.org/files/programs/douglass/speech_complete.pdf.

much of what they loved. These prophets called on them to hope for more than a destruction of their foes and the salvation of Israel. Shockingly, they look to the salvation of their former enemies:

> It is too light a thing that you should be my servant
>> to raise up the tribes of Jacob
>> and to restore the survivors of Israel;
> I will give you as a light to the nations,
>> that my salvation may reach to the end of the earth. (Is 49:6)[9]

These passages have become so commonplace that the deep challenge they propose to Israel might be lost to us if they are not read with Psalm 137 ringing in our ears. Texts such as Psalm 137 speak to the anger that we rightly feel because of the wrongs done to us. Yet these prophetic texts call us to the costly and painful work of imagining a world beyond our grievances. This does not rule out justice; it speaks to what happens afterward. And what happens afterward will matter if there is more to the African American future than us replacing our oppressors and doing the same thing to them that they did to us.

Passages such as Isaiah 2:2-5 envision a deep forgiveness not easily imaginable within the narrative world of Isaiah because he also looks forward to the destruction of Babylon. There is a tension within Isaiah. God must be just, and he must judge sin. But there must also be more. The most hopeful places within Isaiah's narrative occur during its descriptions of the coming son of David.

When Isaiah turns to his description of the king, it all comes together (Is 11:1-10). We find the wisdom of God, the establishment of justice, and even the end of hostility between animals and humanity. War and death meet a foe more powerful: the king. Most importantly, the nations of the world begin to view this king as a

---

[9]See also Zech 8:20-23; Is 2:2-5.

rallying point. What brings the warring parties of the world together is not the emergence of a new philosophy of government; it
is not free market capitalism, communism, socialism, or democracy.
It is a person: the root of Jesse. Isaiah then calls for Black people, in
the midst of their pain, to begin to envision a world not defined by
our anger. The Bible calls on us to develop a theological imagination
within which we can see the world as a community and not a collection of hostilities. It does so by giving us the vision of a person
who can heal our wounds and dismantle our hostilities.

THE CROSS BREAKS THE WHEEL

It is possible to read the Old Testament and privilege passages such
as Psalm 137 over Isaiah 11:1-10. It is possible to skip over the middle
portion of the New Testament and turn immediately to John's apocalypse where the enemies of God's people experience fiery judgment.
The picture of God judging wickedness is not an idea reserved for
the Old Testament. The meek and mild Jesus of popular imagination
is the creation of the comfortable middle class. The oppressed know
Jesus as the rider upon the white horse whose robe is dipped in the
blood of his enemies (Rev 19:11-14). But if there is a miracle (that's
often criticized) of Black Christianity, it is that we have been profoundly influenced by the themes of forgiveness and the multiethnic
community that fill the pages of the New Testament. We have found
our way there by means of the cross.

Let me be clear. The cross of Jesus Christ is not an intellectual
apologetic that allows Black Christians to say that we now understand the whip and chain in the wider scope of God's purposes. We
do not believe that our slavery was intended for the salvation of
America. We do not hold to some broken and distorted application
of Joseph's story (Gen 50:19-21). No, what happened to the enslaved

and their descendants in this country was and remains an unmitigated evil. But how does God respond to our cries?

He does not respond in a series of syllogisms rooted either in the freedom of the will or the majesty of his sovereignty. In other words, God does not say to us that because there is free will some people will abuse that free will and do evil things like slavery. That might be one intellectual defense of evil in the Christian tradition, but historically that has not been the means by which Black Christians processed our oppression. Neither has God often responded to us in the way that he responded to Job, merely by revealing his sovereign glory and silencing our questions. God in his mercy has allowed us to continue to voice our complaints.

On this side of the passion and resurrection, Black anger and pain is answered personally, by the truly human one. We have found solace in the fact that God responds to Black suffering with a profound act of identification with our suffering. I speak of Jesus, of an identification with the human condition that compels us:

> Who, being in the form of God, did not consider equality with God
> something to be grasped, but emptied himself, taking the form of a slave
> in the likeness of humanity. And being found in the form of a human,
> he humbled himself, becoming obedient unto death, even death upon
> a cross. (Phil 2:6-8, my translation)

What is God's first answer to Black suffering (and the wider human suffering and the rage that comes alongside it)? It is to enter that suffering alongside us as a friend and a redeemer. The answer to Black rage is the calming words of the Word made flesh. The incarnation that comes all the way down, even unto death, has been enough for us to say yes, God, we trust you.

We have decided to trust God because he knows what it means to be at the mercy of a corrupt state that knows little of human rights.

Rome and the antebellum South may not be twins, but they are definitely close relatives, maybe even siblings of the same father. On the cross we meet a God who experienced injustice in the flesh. Seen from one angle, the cross shows that God in Christ knows and understands the plight of the innocent suffers of the world.

But what reaches out and grabs the heart of the Black Christian is not simply that Christ was innocent of the charges levied against him. If that were the full message of the cross, Jesus would merely be another in a long line of martyrs. Jesus stands out as the truly innocent sufferer who had done nothing wrong.

We are not slave owners. Nonetheless, we have in ways large and small participated in the harm of others. We have also damaged ourselves and rebelled against our Creator. The results have come back from the analysis of the human condition and the data is clear: we are all sinners. Jesus is not. The Christian tradition says that the innocent one suffered for us individually and corporately to bring us to God (Gal 2:20; Rom 4:25). The profound act of mercy gives us the theological resources to forgive. We forgive because we have been forgiven. It is only by looking at our enemies through the lens of the cross that we can begin to imagine the forgiveness necessary for community. What do Black Christians do with the rage that we rightly feel? We send it to the cross of Christ.

Justo González, in his important work *Mañana*, makes a compelling case that the United States must come to grips with what it did to Mexico. In making this claim he does not render Mexico completely innocent. Instead he quotes the proverb *"Ladrón que roba a ladrón ha cien años de perdón"* ("A thief who robs a thief has a hundred years' pardon").[10] González was not making a moral equivalence between

---

[10]Justo L. González, *Mañana: Christian Theology from a Hispanic Perspective* (Nashville: Abingdon Press, 1990), 32.

all acts of evil nor was he claiming that it is improper to attempt to right wrongs. He was saying that if you dig deep enough into any people's corporate or personal past, you will find wrong. In Christian theology this plays out in the words of Paul: "All have sinned and fall short of the glory of God" (Rom 3:23 NIV). It is only by remembering that God's forgiveness costs him something that I find the divinely given power to pay the cost of forgiveness instead of revenge. The sword gives birth to the sword, but the cross breaks the wheel.

The claim that the cross breaks the wheel and that costly forgiveness is possible is not unique to the African American context; is it also the story of first-century Israel. Jesus calling for an end to rage and the possibility of forgiveness cannot be abstracted from the particularities of the Roman occupation of Judea. Jesus came into a world in which his fellow Jews had every reason to be angry at Rome. They were an occupied country—overtaxed, exploited, and subject to all the indignities of colonial rule. Those in Israel who still hoped for a Messiah often looked for one that would defeat their enemies.[11] Zechariah's psalm, which opens the gospel of Luke, did not portend a passion of the Messiah, but rather his victory (Lk 1:71-79). John the Baptist was so confounded by the ministry of Jesus that he wondered if Jesus was the one or if he should look for another (Lk 7:19). But nonetheless, these early Jewish Christians, who had all the historical ammunition needed to seek the ruin of their Gentile oppressors, made it their mission to convert a largely hostile Roman world.

This call to transform rage into love and forgiveness can be misheard. It can be heard as a means of justifying continued abuse and acquiescing to mistreatment. There are two reasons that willingly

---

[11]On the diversity of Messianic expectation, see Esau McCaulley, *Sharing in the Son's Inheritance* (London: T&T Clark, 2019), 1-46; Matthew V. Novenson, *The Grammar of Messianism: An Ancient Jewish Political Idiom and Its Users* (Oxford, UK: Oxford University Press, 2017), 1-33.

accepting abuse is inappropriate for Christians. First, the theological energy of the Bible is toward *liberation*. The exodus speaks of freedom from slavery and the New Testament speaks in numerous places about freedom from sin. God does not intend for his people to remain in bondage forever. Therefore, it is appropriate for those suffering unjustly to forgive their enemies from a distance if necessary. We do not have to stay. Second, the New Testament also calls on believers to help those who are suffering. James says, "Religion that is pure and undefiled before God, the Father, is this: to care for orphans and widows in their distress, and to keep oneself unstained by the world" (Jas 1:27). How could we offer those being abused anything less than the end of their suffering when we have the power to grant it? James does not say, "Tell the orphans and the widows to put up with suffering." He says to the Christian, "Help them!" Therefore, finding a place of forgiveness does not mean that we must allow suffering to continue indefinitely when we have the resources to do something about it.

THE RESURRECTION AND THE FINAL JUDGMENT
AS NECESSARY ADDENDUMS

It would be dishonest to say that the account above is always emotionally satisfying. There are times when I look at the present and the historic suffering of my people and I feel closer to Psalm 137 than Luke 23:34 ("Father, forgive them"). That is fine because I am not yet fully formed into the likeness of Christ, and Psalm 137 is a part of the canon for a reason. This side of the second coming there will continue to be Babylons. As long as there is a Babylon, the oppressed will weep beside its willows.

Nonetheless, it is precisely when the wooing of the cross feels its weakest that I must do the hard work of asking myself the most important of questions. Is Christianity a hypothesis or a method of approaching the world? Did the Messiah provide us with a philosophy like Socrates or Nas? If Christianity is mere method, a way of approaching reality, then it is inadequate; but if Christ is risen, trampling down death by death, then the world is a different place even when I do not experience it as such. Paul says it perfectly:

> Now if Christ is proclaimed as raised from the dead, how can some of you say there is no resurrection of the dead? If there is no resurrection of the dead, then Christ has not been raised; and if Christ has not been raised, then our proclamation has been in vain and your faith has been in vain. We are even found to be misrepresenting God, because we testified of God that he raised Christ—whom he did not raise if it is true that the dead are not raised. For if the dead are not raised, then Christ has not been raised. If Christ has not been raised, your faith is futile and you are still in your sins. Then those also who have died in Christ have perished. If for this life only we have hoped in Christ, we are of all people most to be pitied. (1 Cor 15:12-19)

Without the resurrection, the forgiveness embedded in the cross is the wistful dream of a pious fool. But I am convinced that the Messiah has defeated death. I can forgive my enemies because I believe the resurrection happened. I am convinced the God who had the power to judge me did not. Instead he invited me into communion with his Son and through that union with the Messiah I discover the resources to love that I did not possess before. When anger is victorious in my own heart it never defeats God.

Belief in the resurrection requires us to believe that nothing is impossible. If death gives way to the power of God, so does my hate. But more than that, resurrection is the final vindication of all Black hopes and dreams. If Black anger arises from the disregard of Black bodies and the failure to see us as persons, then resurrected Black and Brown bodies are God's final affirmation of our value. When God finally calls the dead to life, he calls them to life with their ethnic identity intact (Rev 7:9).

And yet, Christianity does teach that all will have to give an account for their actions. The final judgment is a source of terrifying comfort. John's apocalypse recounts a scene when the saints who had been martyred ask a question, "Sovereign Lord, holy and true, how long will it be before you judge and avenge our blood on the inhabitants of the earth?" (Rev 6:10). John does not respond with, "There will be no reckoning." Instead he says that the time has not yet come. John later speaks of the end in which Babylon is judged for its misdeeds (Rev 18:21-24). God will judge wickedness. The sins that have been committed against us matter. This is both terrifying (I find it difficult to long for such an outcome even for my enemies) and comforting (because sin is judged). God's terrible power to judge makes me long for everyone to take advantage of God's offer of forgiveness. Christian eschatology breeds compassion. Many years into my Christian life I still feel the anger, but the cross and the reality of God's power have changed me. I want the oppressor to repent and find healing. I want him or her to be free as well. My rage, then, has hints of sympathy that linger in the back of my most heated moments.

CONCLUSION

It is difficult for the African American believer to look deeply into the history of Christianity and not be profoundly shaken. Insomuch as it arises in response to the church's historic mistreatment of African Americans, the Black secular protest against religion is one of the most understandable developments in the history of the West. If they are wrong (and they are), it is a wrongness born out of considerable pain. I too am frustrated with the way that Scripture has been used to justify the continual assault on Black bodies and souls. If we come to different conclusions about the solutions to those problems, it is not because Black Christians deny the past. It is simply that we found different solutions within the biblical witness to Black suffering and anger. We do not find fault with the broad center of the great Christian tradition. We lament its distortion by others and the ways in which we have failed to live up to the truths we hold dear. Nonetheless, we are not ashamed of finding hope and forgiveness in and through the cross of Christ. In the end, we plead and have confidence in the blood.

SEVEN

THE FREEDOM OF THE SLAVES

PENNINGTON'S TRIUMPH

■ ■ ■

Do you talk of selling a man? You might as well
talk of selling immortality or sunshine.
LEONARD BLACK

The LORD said, "I have indeed seen the misery of my people in Egypt.
I have heard them crying out because of their slave drivers,
and I am concerned about their suffering. So I
have come down to rescue them."
EXODUS 3:7-8

I REMEMBER THE PRIDE THAT I FELT when I told my mother I had
read the entire Bible from cover to cover. Earlier that summer, she had
bought me a comic book version of the Scriptures that recounted the
major epochs of the biblical story from Genesis to Revelation. I must
have read the pastorals, but they were unable to touch me. My imagination was captured by the God of the exodus who called a people to

freedom from slavery. I grew up hearing about a God who looked upon the suffering of his Black and Brown children with righteous indignation. For me the Bible was a source of hope. Nonetheless, we grow and change. The text grows in complexity as we do. Eventually, I came across Paul's words to slaves. The weight of the legacy of slavery in the United States landed in full force upon my imagination:

> Let all who are under the yoke of slavery regard their masters as worthy of all honor, so that the name of God and the teaching may not be blasphemed. Those who have believing masters must not be disrespectful to them on the ground that they are members of the church; rather they must serve them all the more, since those who benefit by their service are believers and beloved. (1 Tim 6:1-2)

In the hands of white slave owners, the Bible was a tool of oppression. In my first mature pass through Paul, I wondered if they might be right. This passage seems to tell enslaved persons to content themselves with their station. This is exactly how these passages were used to justify slavery in the United States.[1]

What are we to make of Paul's legacy? Some African Americans have dealt with it by avoiding Paul. But the question is simply too urgent to set aside. Some 130 years before my birth, the Black pastor and abolitionist James W. C. Pennington put words to our anxiety:

> Does the Bible condemn slavery without any regard to circumstances or not? I, for one, desire to know. My repentance, my faith, my hope, my love, my perseverance all all, I conceal it not, I repeat it, all turn upon this point. If I am deceived here—if the word of God does sanction slavery, I want another book, another repentance, another faith, and another hope![2]

---

[1] Allen Dwight Callahan, *The Talking Book: African Americans and the Bible* (New Haven, CT: Yale University Press, 2006), 32.

[2] Quoted in James Cone, *The Cross and the Lynching Tree* (Maryknoll, NY: Orbis, 2013), 27.

The question for Pennington was not whether this verse or that verse condones slavery. His questions revolve around the character of God. If the Bible supported the kidnapping of Black bodies, the rape of Black men and women, the separation of families, the whip and the chain, then he needed another *book* altogether. He needed another faith and another hope. In a sense the question behind all questions for the Black Christians is this one. Did God intend our freedom? Our reflections on the Bible and the Black Christian then should end here at the origin of all our problems, the question of the Bible and slavery.

Asking about slavery in the way that Pennington does with 1 Timothy 6:1-3 in the canon appears to risk too much. It seems to risk the resurrection. On first glance, it puts the communion of saints, the Eucharist, and the gathering of every tribe and nation in danger. It can feel like a reckless form of inquiry. But we must press into it. Does the Bible sanction what happened to Black bodies on this continent?

On the first read, the Bible does not appear to say all that we want it to say in the way that we want the Bible to say it. And yet this is the crucial part: *the Bible says more than enough.* The story of Christianity does not on every page legislate slavery out of existence. Nonetheless, the Christian narrative, our core theological principles, and our ethical imperatives create a world in which slavery becomes unimaginable. The Bible, taken in its entirety, remains a light in a dark and broken world. It is their fault that slave masters took so long to walk out of darkness and into the light. To make this case, I want to begin by highlighting how Jesus' interpretive method allows us to state plainly that God didn't intend our slavery. Then we will examine select Old and New Testament texts that allow us to imagine a world with God as king and slavery ended.

BIBLE READING, SLAVERY, AND GOD'S PURPOSES

Toward the end of Jesus' earthly ministry, he found himself in constant conflict with his opponents as he journeyed toward Jerusalem (Mt 16:21; Lk 24:25-27). On one occasion, the Pharisee came to question him on divorce, an issue seemingly a world away from our subject of slavery. It is worth quoting in full:

> Some Pharisees came to him, and to test him they asked, "Is it lawful for a man to divorce his wife for any cause?" He answered, "Have you not read that the one who made them at the beginning 'made them male and female,' and said, 'For this reason a man shall leave his father and mother and be joined to his wife, and the two shall become one flesh'? So they are no longer two, but one flesh. Therefore what God has joined together, let no one separate." They said to him, "Why then did Moses command us to give a certificate of dismissal and to divorce her?" He said to them, "It was because you were so hard-hearted that Moses *allowed* you to divorce your wives, but *from the beginning it was not so.*" (Mt 19:3-8, emphasis added)

The Pharisees wanted Jesus to interpret Deuteronomy 24:1-4 and other parts of the Torah that dealt with the question of divorce. They had no plans of debating the practice of divorce, but rather the circumstances of its application. Here the divorce question is similar to the slave question as it was handled by the slave masters of the antebellum South. They maintained that the options were biblical slavery versus bad slavery. The problem was not slavery itself, which had strong biblical support, but the excesses of a few.

Many scholars have discussed the seemingly hard stance against divorce that Jesus presents here. That is not my concern. My focus is on the exegetical reasoning that he uses to make his case. He does not engage the text that his opponents have in mind—Deuteronomy 24:1-4. Instead, he turns to the opening words of Genesis. He speaks about God's *creational intent.* The question, for Jesus, is not what the Torah *allows,* but what God *intended.*

Jesus argued that before the fall there was no divorce and therefore we were not made for divorce. Instead man and woman were made to enjoy each other forever. This seems to leave his opponents stunned. Why have these passages at all? Jesus replies that Moses instituted these laws because of their hardness of heart. He wanted them to remember that "it was not this way from the beginning."

Jesus' argument here suggests that the norms for Christian ethics are not the passages that are allowances for human sin, such as Moses' divorce laws. What matters is what we were made to be. Jesus shows that not every passage of the Torah presents the ideal for human interactions. Instead some passages accept the world as broken and attempt to limit the damage that we do to one another. This means that when we look at the passages in the Old Testament we have to ask ourselves about their purpose. Do they present a picture of what God wanted us to be or do they seek to limit the damage arising from a broken world?

Paul speaks in a similar way when he says that the law was instituted because of sin and functioned as our guardian until the coming of Christ (Gal 3:19-24). This does not mean that the law is bad (Gal 3:21), nor does it dismiss the formative role that the law played on Christian ethics. But it does mean that sometimes the law limits the damage that we do to one another.

So we come to the most urgent of questions right away. When we turn to the opening of Genesis and look at the creation account is there any evidence that God *intended* the descendants of Adam and Eve to enslave one another or is slavery a manifestation of the fall? If slavery is a result of the fall, then it is false to claim that God's will is slavery. It is also false to claim that the Bible presents slavery as a good thing for Black people. Slavery is always and forever wrapped in sin. One way to see this is to turn our eyes from Genesis and move toward Revelation. What is God's vision for the reconciliation of all things (Rev 21:3-4)? It is a community of the healed and transformed, not the enslaved. If Christian ethics is about living now in light of the coming future, then the coming future freedom of all people has to at some point become flesh in the formerly enslaved bodies whose very *physical* freedom is an enacted parable of the gospel.

I want to contend that the Old Testament and later the New Testament create an imaginative world in which slavery becomes more and more untenable. Stated differently, God created a people who could theologically deconstruct slavery. We rightly have complaints that it seemed to take some 1,800 years before a significant number of Christians came to this conclusion. We do have to recognize that Christians began to make strong theological cases against slavery as early as the fourth century in a way that would stand out among their non-Christian peers.[3] What is even more interesting is that no society that preceded the eighteenth-century abolitions contended that slavery itself was fundamentally immoral. The widespread move to abolish slavery is a Christian innovation.

THE OLD TESTAMENT AND GOD'S CHARACTER: A SECOND OVERTURE

I argued that Jesus makes a distinction within the Torah between passages that articulate God's purposes (creation account) and those that limit the impact of human sin (divorce laws). When he was making ethical judgments, then, Jesus did not begin with the

---

[3]Tom Holland, *Dominion: How the Christian Revolution Remade the World* (New York: Basic Books, 2019), 141-42; Stuart G. Hall, *Gregory of Nyssa: Homilies on Ecclesiastes: An English Version with Supporting Studies*, Proceedings of the Seventh International Colloquium on Gregory of Nyssa (Berlin: De Gruyter, 1993), 177-84.

allowances and reason from there. He called people to remember their creational purposes. I argue a similar logic should be used with the Old Testament slavery laws.

Now I want to pursue the slave question from a slightly different angle, namely slavery and God's character. Here again I follow Pennington, who says,

> Much is attempted to be made of the fact that men in other ages have been slaveholders. . . . But the question is not affected by what the Bible records as matter-of-fact history, but only by what it reveals as consistent or inconsistent with the moral nature of God, what is obedient or rebellious before his throne.[4]

In effect he is saying, What does the Bible reveal about God's character? Does God appear to take pleasure in slavery?

The exodus narrative is definitive in this regard. What is God like? He is a God who hears the sufferings of an enslaved people and rescues them (Ex 3:7-10). This rescue becomes a part of his résumé (Deut 7:8; Lev 11:45). When the Israelites prayed to God, they prayed to a God whose character was revealed in his liberating activity. God's liberating character was to be reflected in Israel's attitude toward outsiders (Deut 24:17). There is a theological link, then, from the compassion of Israel to the very character of God. We are so used to this Old Testament story that the exodus has lost it power. We have been trained in slaveholder exegesis, where the limits on sin have transformed into the ideal and the stories have been sapped of their strength.

The enslaved Black Christians knew. No fancy exegetical moves could convince them that the God who liberated the Israelites didn't care about enslaved persons in this country:

---

[4]James W. C. Pennington, *A two years' absence, or, A farewell sermon, preached in the Fifth Congregational Church, Nov. 2, 1845* (Hartford, CT: H. T. Wells, 1845).

Aunt Jane used to tell us, too, that the children of Israel was in Egypt in bondage, and that God delivered them out of Egypt; and she said he would deliver us. We all used to sing a hymn like this:

"He delivered Daniel from the lions' den,

Jonah from the belly of the whale,

The three Hebrew children from the fiery furnace,

And why not deliver me too?"[5]

The enslaved people read (or heard) in the biblical texts about a God who delighted in liberation, and this gave them hope. It was not that the slave passages didn't exist; they simply couldn't be used to undo the testimony of the exodus. When they turned to the biblical texts, they didn't see God describing himself as the God who enslaves people and therefore his chosen nation should enslave others. Instead they saw in the stories of Daniel, Moses, and Jonah a much different God than the one described by their slave masters.

IS THE DEVIL IN THE DETAILS? SOME
OLD TESTAMENT SLAVE TEXTS

The early Black exegetical tradition was correct. God's character speaks against slavery. But do we see examples of Jesus' exegetical distinction between texts that articulate God's intent and those that limit sin? Does the Torah (in places) attempt to limit the damage caused by the sin of slavery? The only way to answer that question is to look at slavery as it is depicted in some texts of the Torah. It would be impossible in the space that we have to do justice to all the Old Testament slave passages, metaphors, and narratives. The biblical world was one in which slavery was the norm and the Bible

---

[5]Octavia V. Rogers Albert, *The house of bondage or Charlotte Brooks and other slaves original and life-like, as they appeared in their old plantation and city slave life; together with pen-pictures of the peculiar institution, with sights and insights into their new relations as freedmen, freemen, and citizens* (New York: Hunt and Eaton, 1890), 31.

reflects that reality.[6] Nonetheless, it is important to sketch some of the ways in which the Old Testament deals with this reality.

An important caveat is needed. I am not arguing that the Bible depicts "good slavery" and then contrasts that with the "bad slavery" of the North American slave trade. I am not arguing that slavery in the Bible was different from the North American slave trade and *for that reason* the biblical account loses its sting. Thus, I am not going to sketch out the differences between ancient Near Eastern slavery and American chattel slavery. That information is readily available.[7] Instead, I am wondering whether the Bible gives us space to hope that God intends freedom for all people. I think that the Bible does give us room for hope. I am going to discuss three reasons: (1) the practice of manumitting Hebrew slaves; (2) some rules around mistreatment of slaves; and (3) the sanctuary given to runaway slaves.

In Israel, no Hebrew slave could be enslaved for more than six years, and when the slave was freed he or she was to be given resources to start a new life:

> If a member of your community, whether a Hebrew man or a Hebrew woman, is sold to you and works for you six years, in the seventh year you shall set that person free. And when you send a male slave out from you a free person, you shall not send him out empty-handed. Provide liberally out of your flock, your threshing floor, and your wine press, thus giving to him some of the bounty with which the LORD your God has blessed you. Remember that you were a slave in the land of Egypt, and the LORD your God redeemed you; for this reason I lay this command upon you today. (Deut 15:12-15)

---

[6]Pennington, *Two Years' Absence*, 23.

[7]For a fuller discussion of slavery in the ANE, see S. S. Bartchy, "Slavery," in *The International Standard Bible Encyclopedia (Revised)*, ed. Geoffery W. Bromiley, Accordance electronic edition, version 1.2 (Grand Rapids, MI: Eerdmans, 1979), 539-47; G. H. Haas, "Slave, Slavery" in *Dictionary of Old Testament: Pentateuch*, ed. T. Desmond Alexander and David W. Baker (Downers Grove, IL: InterVarsity Press, 2003).

Hebrew Bible scholar Jacob Milgrom says that this passage "virtually abolishes the institution of slavery."[8] There is no comparable law with this scope or generosity in the ancient Near East.[9]

The point here is not mere compassion. Manumission was rooted in a specific call to imitate what God did for Israel. Biblical scholar Peter Craigie says, "They were to remember that, when they had been slaves, God had loved them, freed them, and made ample provision for them; as sons of God."[10]

I wish that the account of slavery ended there, but the promise to liberate did not extend to enslaved foreigners (Lev 25:39-46). Does this represent a form of implicit racism in which it becomes possible to enslave foreigners because they are seen as less than fully human?

This denial of Black humanity undergirded the American slave trade. James Henry Hammond, senator of South Carolina, said the following during a speech before the senate in 1858:

> In all social systems there must be a class to do the menial duties, to perform the drudgery of life. . . . Fortunately for the South, she found a race adapted to that purpose to her hand. A race inferior to her own, but eminently qualified in temper, in vigor, in docility, in capacity to stand the climate, to answer all her purposes.[11]

[8]Jacob Milgrom, *Leviticus 23–27*, Anchor Bible 3b (New York: Doubleday, 2001), 2214.
[9]Milgrom, *Leviticus 23–27*, 2214.
[10]Peter C. Craigie, *The Book of Deuteronomy*, NICOT (Grand Rapids, MI: Eerdmans, 1976), 239. See also Mark Rooker who says, "The fact that the servitude of the Israelites has a negative connotation is evident from the frequent warning that the period of slavery was not to be characterized by severity (25:43, 46, 53), which may suggest that there is something intrinsically incongruous about the institution of slavery." Mark F. Rooker, *Leviticus*, ed. E. Ray Clendenen and Kenneth A. Mathew, NAC 3a (Nashville: Broadman & Holman Publishers, 2000), 310.
[11]See also Albert Beverage justifying the United States annexation of the Philippines: "We will not renounce our part in the mission of the race, trustee, under God, of the civilization of the world. . . . He has made us the master organizers of the world to establish system when chaos reigns." Larry G. Murphy, "Evil and Sin in African American Theology," in *The Oxford Handbook of African American Theology*, ed. Katie G. Cannon and Anthony B. Pinn (Oxford, UK: Oxford University Press, 2014), 212-27.

His words are important because American slavery was not rooted in a detached reading of biblical texts. Instead the biblical text was read in light of an anthropology growing out of blatant racism, lust, and greed.

Why didn't the laws of Jubilee apply to foreign slaves? When God redeemed Israel from slavery, they became his people and for that reason none of his people could unwillingly be made permanent slaves again. He also promised his people the land of Israel. Even when poverty forced them into slavery a hope of return remained. Jubilee existed to ensure that reality.[12]

Even though enslaved foreigners did not participate in Jubilee, there are other places to turn to for hope. One source is the eschatological vision of peace and learning depicted in the prophets. There were two main causes of slavery in the ancient Near East: debt and war.[13] But the coming eschatological kingdom of God as predicted in Isaiah looks to the end of war and to material abundance (Is 2:2-4; 25:6). The end of war and the end of scarcity carries with it the end of slavery because slavery grows out of lack and violence.

The prophets look to more than the end of war. They look to the spread of the law to the Gentiles:

> Many peoples shall come and say,
> "Come, let us go up to the mountain of the Lord,
>   to the house of the God of Jacob;
>   that he may teach us his ways
>   and that we may walk in his paths."
> For out of Zion shall go forth instruction,
>   and the word of the Lord from Jerusalem. (Is 2:3)

---

[12]Milgrom, *Leviticus 23–27*, 2231.
[13]Haas, "Slave, Slavery."

The law going forth from Zion (Jerusalem) is linked to the vocation of Israel. When God promised to bless Israel, it was for the specific purpose of blessing the world. The idea was that the nations around Israel would see the wonderful things that God was doing for Israel and decide to emulate them. This is why they were to come to Israel and learn God's ways. If we take that passage seriously, if the nations were supposed to adopt the Torah, that would in effect eliminate permanent slavery (due to the six-year manumission law) in all those nations and create an ever-expanding place of refuge for enslaved people.[14] When reflecting on manumission laws, God's justice becoming "a light to the nations" takes on real significance (Is 51:4). Israel's purpose was to show that there was a better way to order their societies and in so doing positively influence the nations around them. In other words, the vision for the freedom of enslaved Israelites and the laws governing that freedom should have functioned as a witness.

Is this all that the enslaved foreigner could hope for? No. There are two other ways in which the slave laws in Israel testified to God's vision for a slave-free world. The first is the rule for runaway slaves, and the second is the provision of some protections for enslaved persons. We will consider the runaway rules briefly before turning to an important series of passages in Exodus on the treatment of enslaved persons.

> Slaves who have escaped to you from their owners shall not be given back to them. They shall reside with you, in your midst, in any place they choose in any one of your towns, wherever they please; you shall not oppress them. (Deut 23:15-16)

---

[14]See the discussion on runaways below.

This law again was without precedent in the ancient Near East or the Greco-Roman world in Jesus' day.[15] In theory, enslaved persons outside of Israel could see Israel as a place of safety.[16] As written this text also seems to allow fleeing within Israel from one part of the country to another to escape slavery. Therefore, although the law allowed Israelites to maintain foreign slaves, it never mandated *any slave* to stay in that condition if they could escape. In other words, the exodus lingered in the background. I know of no other culture that said in effect to slaves, if you can get free there will be help for you.

Thus far, I have argued that the character of God as revealed in the exodus narrative and the compassion that it was to inspire provides us with the imaginative tools to think theologically about a world without slavery. I then claimed that the Hebrew slave manumission laws were linked to the land promise and allowed all Israelites to maintain a share in the inheritance. Finally, I argued that the limitation of the Jubilee laws to Israelites strikes us as a hard word, but that it wasn't rooted in the same anthropological distinctions that undergirded the American slave trade. In addition, I claim that the vision for the universal application of the law among the nations carries with it universal abolition. Furthermore, in contrast to about every other society of its day, the Torah promised freedom to any enslaved person that managed to escape their masters.

The last element of our Old Testament discussion will focus on the treatment of slaves. Exodus 21:20-21 is translated in the NIV as:

---

[15]Duane L. Christensen, *Deuteronomy 21:10–34:12*, WBC 6B (Grand Rapids, MI: Zondervan, 2002), 549, says, "this command runs contrary to all known ancient Near Eastern law codes, which forbade the harboring of runaway slaves."

[16]"The choice granted to a slave to take up residence in any of Israel's cities exhibits a considerable degree of personal freedom," Ronald E. Clements, "The Book of Deuteronomy," in *Numbers-2 Samuel*, NIB 2 (Nashville: Abingdon Press, 1998), 462.

Anyone who beats their male or female slave with a rod must be punished if the slave dies as a direct result, but they are not to be punished
if the slave recovers after a day or two, since the slave is their property.

This passage seems to treat the death of the enslaved person as something akin to a minor crime that leads to a punishment such as a
fine.[17] Most other translations think the same.[18]

However, many scholars have noted that the word translated punished usually does not merely mean "punish." It means "avenge."[19]
This passage shows that the Old Testament did not see the enslaved
person as mere property whose life had no value. Instead a murder
of a slave, was just that; a murder of a human being made in God's
image. This passage does not say who does the avenging. I am convinced that given the possibility that an enslaved foreigner would
lack kinsmen to avenge him that it fell to God.[20]

Does this mean that one could beat an enslaved person nearly to
death and as long as the enslaved person lives, the owner would not
be liable to punishment? Exodus 21:26-27 suggests otherwise:

When a slaveowner strikes the eye of a male or female slave, de-
stroying it, the owner shall let the slave go, a free person, to compensate for the eye. If the owner knocks out a tooth of a male or
female slave, the slave shall be let go, a free person, to compensate for
the tooth.

While this passage sadly does not eliminate all forms of abuse, it does
say that any injury to the slave, including the loss of a tooth, results

---

[17]See the discussion in William H. C. Propp, *Exodus 19–40: A New Translation with Introduction and Commentary*, Anchor Bible (New York: Doubleday, 2006), 219.

[18]See also NRSV, NAB, NJKV, NET.

[19]Nahum M. Sarna, *Exodus*, The JPS Torah Commentary (Philadelphia: The Jewish Publication Society, 1991), 124; Victor P. Hamilton, *Exodus: An Exegetical Commentary* (Grand
Rapids, MI: Baker Academic, 2011), 384.

[20]See Hamilton, *Exodus*, 384. Sarna, *Exodus*, 124, suggests that the community executed
the criminal.

in freedom. No other ancient Near Eastern text treated an enslaved person as an agent capable of being wronged.[21] The Bible makes the unheard-of claim that the enslaved person goes free because of the loss of "his tooth" or "his eye."[22] The body of the slave remains her body not the body of her master. Injury to that body requires that the *slave* receive redress.

I am not arguing that the biblical text depicts easy slavery while American slaves had it worse. The question I wanted to pursue was whether the biblical texts condoned slavery as good or whether it sought to limit the damages of a broken world. Reading and interpreting these passages as a descendant of slaves remains painful. Maybe the healing of those wounds is eschatological. Nonetheless, while we wish that some Old Testament texts would go further, it is to my mind clear that God's very character and the central story of the Old Testament speaks against slavery. Slavery is a manifestation of the fall, and God begins the story of Israel by freeing them from slavery as a symbol of hope. My ancestors read it that way and so do I. The Old Testament laws recognize the humanity and dignity of the enslaved person in ways that far outstrip Israel's contemporaries. It also provides various avenues for freedom. It is not everything, but it is enough, because I can follow the trajectory of these texts toward liberation.

AND FINALLY, THE APOSTLE PAUL

But what of the apostle Paul, who's presented to Black Christians as the fount of all our troubles? No one in Paul's day or in the centuries that follow ever seemed to envision the end of slavery as an institution.[23] Paul doesn't appear to believe that his small

---

[21]Sarna, *Exodus*, 127.

[22]I am grateful to Aubrey Buster, Old Testament professor at Wheaton College, for pointing this out to me in private conversation.

[23]The notable exception being Gregory of Nyssa. See Tom Holland, *Dominion: How the Christian Revolution Remade the World* (New York: Basic Books, 2019), 141-42.

and fledging communities could do anything so dramatic as to change Roman Law. Nonetheless, I want to see whether there are aspects of Paul's thought that provide the tools to imagine a world on the other side of slavery. This quest is not unbiased or completely thorough. I will only deal with three Pauline texts as examples of the ways in which he does provide the resources to see the enslaved differently. These are his letter to Philemon, 1 Timothy 6:1-3, and 1 Corinthians 7:21-24.

Onesimus the escaped slave, and more than was requested. When one thinks of Paul and slavery, eventually we must address the complex narrative of Paul, Onesimus, and Philemon. This is not a theological reflection about an abstract slave and an imagined master. Here we see Paul put his theology into practice. What do texts like 1 Timothy 6:1-3 look like when an enslaved person has escaped?[24]

Slaveholders argued that Paul dutifully returned the slave and used that argument to justify slavery.[25] I want to argue that Paul does two things that undermine slavery in this passage: (1) Paul transforms social relationships and status in light of Christ, and (2) Paul requests that Philemon free Onesimus.[26]

Paul refers to himself and others as prisoners of Jesus Christ (Philem 1, 9, 10, 12, 23). This lower status has the effect of placing

---

[24]Many assume that Onesimus stole from and ran away from Philemon. For an analysis and critique, see Obusitswe Kingsley Tiroyabone, "Reading Philemon with Onesimus in the Postcolony: Exploring a Postcolonial Runaway Slave Hypothesis," *Acta Theologica* 24 (2016): 225-36.

[25]James Noel says, "Seen through this lens of the oppressive discursive structures of their own construction, it is no wonder that white proslavery advocates would read Paul's reference to Onesimus's being made more useful to Paul as something that would unfold within the framework of Onesimus's continued servitude." James A. Noel, "Nat Is Back: The Return of the Re/Oppressed in Philemon," in *Onesimus Our Brother: Reading Religion, Race, and Culture in Philemon*, ed. Matthew V. Johnson, James A. Noel, and Demetrius K. Williams (Minneapolis, MN: Fortress Press, 2012), 73.

[26]Tiroyabone, "Reading Philemon," 231, rightly notes that most readings of Philemon are "colonial" in that they assume "Paul wanted the colonial master-slave relationships to prevail, even in Christian groups, and does not make room for the possibility that Paul would have wanted Onesimus released from the master-slave relationship."

Paul on the same level as Onesimus in the eyes of society.[27] If some were tempted to view Onesimus as a criminal for escaping, they would also be forced to condemn the apostle. Paul, then, does not begin his pastoral intervention from a place of power, but one of weakness. Lloyd A. Lewis says, "Paul's more literal identification of himself by his criminal status places his high profile in the church to the side. Apostleship was not in this case a significant marker of Paul's rank. Philemon, therefore, hears Paul placing himself on a level comparable to that of another criminal and slave."[28]

Paul's rhetoric makes it difficult for Philemon to make much of his status as owner and Onesimus's status as slave.[29] Paul also uses familial language, calling Philemon his bother. The point is clear. Oneness in Christ transforms relationships. Society values those with power and status. Christians treat all people—slave, free, or prisoner—as family.[30] This idea that slaves and masters are family undermines slavery. Who would enslave a brother or a sister?

It's easy to be cynical about this language, especially given some of the paternalistic language that surrounded Black slavery in the South. Nonetheless, Christian theology must be allowed to make its

---

[27]Mary Hinkle Shore, "The Freedom of Three Christians: Paul's Letter to Philemon and the Beginning of a New Age," Word & World 38 (Fall 2018): 390-97, notes that Paul does not mention his apostleship, but highlights his status as prisoner.

[28]Lloyd A. Lewis, "Philemon," in True to Our Native Land: An African American Commentary on the New Testament, ed. Brian K. Blount et al. (Minneapolis, MN: Fortress Press, 2007), 439.

[29]Some have disputed Onesimus's status as a slave arguing instead that he was Philemon's brother. See Allen Dwight Callahan, "Paul's Epistle to Philemon: Toward an Alternative Argumentum," Harvard Theological Review 86, no. 4 (1993): 357-76. For a response, see Margaret M. Mitchell, "John Chrysostom on Philemon: A Second Look," Harvard Theological Review 88, no. 1 (1995): 135-48.

[30]Mitzi J. Smith, "Utility, Fraternity, and Reconciliation: Ancient Slavery as a Context for the Return of Onesimus," in Onesimus Our Brother: Reading Religion, Race, and Culture in Philemon, ed. M. V. Johnson, J. A. Noel, and D. K. Williams (Minneapolis, MN: Fortress, 2012), 47-58, claims—based on the pun on his name, "useless" and now useful, in Philemon 11—that Paul still views Onesimus through the stereotypes of slaves as lazy and dishonest. See however the response by Jennifer A. Glancy, "The Utility of an Apostle: On Philemon 11," Journal of Early Christian History 5, no. 1 (2015): 72-86.

own case. Paul believes that Jesus came in the form of a slave and by doing so brought salvation to the world (Phil 2:15-21). This shaming of those in power through *weakness* is a theme Paul returns to again and again in his letters (1 Cor 1:18-31). According to Paul, Jesus serves as a model for how we interact with one another. This theological inversion of interpersonal power dynamics had an impact on how slaves and masters viewed one another.

This idea of power through weakness rooted in love influences the kind of argument that Paul makes. He says, "For this reason, though I am bold enough in Christ to command you to do your duty, yet I would rather appeal to you on the basis of love" (Philem 1:8-9). Whatever it is Paul wants Philemon to do for Onesimus he wants it to be anchored in the love that they share in Christ, not as a mere command. Paul prefers "to do nothing without [Philemon's] consent," and hopes that in the providence of God, Philemon might receive Onesimus back as "no longer a slave but more than a slave, a beloved brother."

What exactly does Paul suggest here? What is the "command" that Paul is holding back from giving? Is Paul simply saying that he wants Philemon to receive Onesimus back and be *more kind* to him now that his slave is a Christian? Some have maintained that all Paul wants is reconciliation, not manumission. They say this because manumission might not be that important to Onesimus or Paul.[31] I respond that they simply do not take seriously the implications of slavery in culture and the good that freedom does to the human soul.

But what does it mean to say that Paul is confident that Philemon will do "more than I ask"? Paul has already *explicitly* requested that

---

[31]F. F. Bruce, *The Epistles to the Colossians, to Philemon, and to the Ephesians*, NICNT (Grand Rapids, MI: Eerdmans, 1984), 191-202; David W. Pao, *Colossians and Philemon*, ZECNT (Grand Rapids, MI: Zondervan, 2012), 341-55.

Philemon receive Onesimus back as a brother. Brown rightly notes that Paul wants

> a Christian slave owner to defy the conventions: To forgive and receive back into the household a runaway slave; to refuse financial reparation when it is offered, mindful of what one owes to Christ as proclaimed by Paul; to go farther in generosity by freeing the servant; and most important of all from a theological viewpoint to recognize in Onesimus a beloved brother and thus acknowledge his Christian transformation.[32]

Bible scholar James Noel recounts an interesting story about teaching Philemon in the context of a church Bible study. During the study one member asked, "What do you think would have happened if an enslaved person returned to his master and shown him this letter?"[33] Here he is trying to get the congregation to imagine how such an event would have shaken up the church. But the more central question is, what would Onesimus have hoped for? When he walked into the house, what reception did he hope to receive? Recent scholarship has rightly asked us to see Onesimus as an agent capable of acting on his own behalf.[34] Tiroyabone posits the following scenario that takes seriously Onesimus's agency:

> He knew that his master had been converted into the Christian faith, as the entire household was now taking part in worship at the house. He knew that the leader of the evangelistic movement was Paul and that he was in Rome. He then stole from Philemon, because he would not be able to reach Rome without any money to meet Paul. In my

---

[32]Raymond Brown, *An Introduction to the New Testament*, Anchor Bible Reference Library (Yale: Yale University Press, 1997), 506; See also Cain Hope Felder, "The Letter to Philemon," in *2 Corinthians–Philemon*, NIB 11 (Nashville: Abingdon Press, 2000), 898-99.
[33]James A. Noel, "Nat is Back," 87.
[34]M. V. Johnson, J. A. Noel, and D. K. Williams, eds. *Onesimus Our Brother: Reading Religion, Race, and Culture in Philemon* (Minneapolis, MN: Fortress, 2012).

observation, Onesimus knew that the new faith proposed new things that had been unheard of in their time. He wanted to be manumitted and, upon staying with Paul, he proved himself a good worker with the intention that Paul would recommend him for manumission.[35]

I do not think that we have evidence to suggest Onesimus stole from Philemon, but his basic point stands. Nothing in the text prevents us from assuming that he sought Paul out with the intention of being freed and that Paul joins him in that effort. Therefore, we must stop calling him a runaway slave. To call him a runaway centers the opinion of slave holders because when someone runs away, the logical thing is to return them. But Onesimus had no desire to be returned. Onesimus did not run away; *he escaped.*

If Onesimus went to Paul hoping for freedom, he found much more. He was changed by the gospel. This does not mean that he expected less, rather he returned with hopes of freedom and Christian brotherhood. Philemon would have been hard pressed to deny such a hope in light of this letter.

Onesimus's longing for freedom gives other Christians room for hope. Here is an excerpt of an appeal by enslaved Christians to the house of representatives in Massachusetts in 1774:

> Our lives are embittered to us. . . . By our deplorable situation we are rendered incapable of shewing our obedience to Almighty God. How can a slave perform the duties of husband to a wife or a parent to his child? How can a husband leave master to work and cleave to his wife? . . . How can the child obey their parents in all things? There is a great number of us sencear . . . members of the Church of Christ. How can the master and the slave be said to fulfill the command, 'Live in Love let brotherly love contuner [continue] and abound Beare ye one anothers Bordens'? How can the master be said to Bear my

---

[35]Tiroyabone, "Reading Philemon," 233-34.

Borden when he Bears me down with they Have [heavy] chains of slavery and operson against my will and how can we fulfill oure part of duty to him whilst in this condition as we cannot searve our God as we ought in this situation.[36]

These Christians argue that the nature of the Christian life requires their freedom. They cannot fully function as husbands, fathers, wives, and children as slaves. The Christian message, then, has put pressure on the institution. Furthermore, these enslaved people appeal to the very same brotherhood that Paul refers to in Philemon. They maintain that "brotherly love" compels Christians to consider what the institution does to their brothers and sisters in Christ. I contend that God intended to use Paul's familial depiction of Christianity to put exactly that type of pressure on the church to redefine and abolish the institution.

The condition of our calling (1 Cor 7:21–24). From Philemon's house to Corinth. In the seventh chapter of Paul's letter to the Corinthians, Paul turns to a series of questions posed to him about how to live as Christians. These questions address marriage, divorce, circumcision, and singleness. His general advice in all these arenas can be summed up with the following: "Each person should live as a believer in whatever situation the Lord has assigned to them" (1 Cor 7:17). If you were already circumcised when you became a Christian, do not try to change that. If you were married to an unbeliever do not pursue a divorce *because* they are not believers.

Our focus here is his discussion of slavery. He says to the slaves:

Were you a slave when you were called? Don't let it trouble you— *although if you can gain your freedom, do so.* For the one who was a slave when called to faith in the Lord is the Lord's freed person; similarly, the one who was free when called is Christ's slave. You

---

[36]Quoted in Callahan, *Talking Book*, 34.

were bought at a price; do not become slaves of human beings."
(1 Cor 7:21-23 NIV)[37]

It is easy to misunderstand Paul's opening statement that the
Christian shouldn't be troubled by slavery. Does he mean that being
enslaved was not important? That is not what Paul was saying. New
Testament scholars Ciampa and Rosner imagine an enslaved person
asking the question, "Isn't my ability to honor and serve God profoundly compromised by the fact that I live the life of a slave? Isn't
this especially the case where it pertains to living a life of sexual
purity and integrity? Wouldn't I have a better standing with God if
only I were free?"[38] This is the exact problem that the enslaved
people in Massachusetts posed to the legislature. Slavery limits their
Christian practice. Paul's point isn't that this question is *insignificant*.
His point is that enslaved people are not *morally* culpable for the sins
visited upon them by their masters.[39] They are not guilty nor does
God love them less if slavery makes it impossible to follow the com-
mands of Christ fully. This is a pastoral response. Even though Paul
says that slaves are not morally culpable for the sins of their masters,
he does counsel them to obtain their freedom if possible.[40]

---

[37]The exact meaning of the phrase in italics is beyond the scope of this book to address. A
good overview of the options can be seen in Michael Flexsenhar, "Recovering Paul's
Hypothetical Slaves: Rhetoric and Reality in 1 Corinthians 7:21," *Journal for the Study of
Paul and His Letters* 5, no. 1 (2015): 71-88. The classic argument that states that Paul
wanted the Corinthians to gain their freedom if possible is found in Will Deming, "A
Diatribe Pattern in 1 Cor. 7:21-22: A New Perspective on Paul's Directions to Slaves,"
Novum Testamentum 37, no. 2 (1995): 130-37.

[38]Roy E. Ciampa and Brian S. Rosner, *The First Letter to the Corinthians*, PNTC (Grand
Rapids, MI: Eerdmans, 2010), 319.

[39]Ciampa and Rosner, *Corinthians*, 319.

[40]See David E. Garland, *1 Corinthians*, Baker Exegetical Commentary on the New Testament (Grand Rapids, MI: Baker Academic, 2003), 309-13. For a bibliography of recent
scholars who take this position, see Flexsenhar, "Recovering Paul," 73n6. He questions
this consensus in part because he doubts that slaves would be able to choose manumission, and because it was often granted without their having a say in the matter. I think
that purchased manumission was more prominent than he thinks, and that Paul was
saying if you can purchase or in some way gain your freedom, do so.

What are the implications for our understanding of Paul and slavery? Paul doesn't believe that Jew and Gentile and slave and free are relativized in the same way. He tells Gentiles that they are not to be circumcised to please God. He tells the slave to get free if they can. Why? Because he recognizes that slavery places limits upon the believer.[41]

We have to ask how this letter would land in a mixed congregation. We have enslavers listening to Paul tell slaves to gain freedom if they could. Paul's words could have been used to convict the consciences of slave masters so that like Philemon they might act out of love. We must also ask how those in power in a democratic republic should have received this message from Paul. Christians should have become the means by which the enslaved person received their long-sought freedom.

1 Timothy 6:1-3. Is the entire revolution undone by 1 Timothy 6:1-3, where Paul tells slaves to submit to their masters? Many would say yes and would further argue that the revolution never in fact occurred. They would suggest the idealized picture of slaves and masters in the New Testament fails to take the suffering of enslaved persons seriously.[42] They suggest that the New Testament deals in abstractions while slavery existed as a lived thing in which people suffered.

There are a few problems with this criticism. It seems to assume a certain cynicism on the part of Paul, as if he really didn't believe that faith could reconfigure relationships but simply used all the *language of reciprocity and family* to keep enslaved persons in line. This makes it seem as if there were two sides—the proslavery and

---

[41]William Webb, *Slaves, Women, and Homosexuals* (Downers Grove, IL: IVP Academic, 2001), 84, argues that Paul's comments on slavery including 1 Corinthians 7:21-24 are "quietly suggestive" of a way of Christian thinking that precludes slavery. He maintains that they set a redemptive trajectory that allows Christians to support abolition.

[42]Anders Martinsen, "Was There New Life for the Social Dead in Early Christian Communities? An Ideological-Critical Interpretation of Slavery in the Household Codes," *Journal of Early Christian History* 2, no. 1 (2012): 55-69.

the abolitionist—and Paul chose the former. There was no wholesale resistance to slavery in Paul's day. Slavery didn't need Paul to maintain it. It was an all-encompassing self-sustaining system. Second, all Christian theology deals with ideals, not just the discussion of slavery. Paul's discussion of the fruit of the Spirit or the mutual love that should mark the Christian life can also be dismissed as idealistic. Nonetheless, Paul believed that such a love was possible even if the church failed repeatedly. We have every reason to believe that Paul believed what he wrote about the church as family and thought that the cross really did reconfigure all social relationships.[43]

But what about what Paul actually says in 1 Timothy 6:1-3? He imagines two scenarios. First, he refers to slaves who have unbelieving masters. He says that they should honor their masters so that God's name and Christian teaching shouldn't be slandered. This portion of his instruction alludes to the passages in the Old Testament that refer to the Gentiles blaspheming God's name because of the poor witness of Israel.[44]

This allusion to an enslaved witness to unbelievers is a much-neglected aspect of 1 Timothy 6:1-3. We have Old Testament examples of what it looks like for enslaved Jews to honor God's name before unbelievers; for example, Daniel and Joseph. In both cases they found themselves under a foreign entity who had power over life and death. Joseph, when pressured to have sex with Potiphar's wife, refused and suffered as a result. Daniel refuses to bow down to an idol. Both were lauded in the biblical and Second Temple material as examples of faithfulness *under slavery*.

---

[43]See N. T. Wright, *Paul and the Faithfulness of God* (Minneapolis, MN: Fortress Press, 2013), 6, on our denial that Paul could actually think revolutionary thoughts.

[44]Philip H. Towner, *The Letters to Timothy and Titus*, NICNT (Grand Rapids, MI: Eerdmans, 2006), 380-81.

Thus, it is wrong to construe Paul's call to submit as implying that he wanted Christian slaves to do whatever their masters wanted. There were examples in the *biblical text* of resisting the sexual advances of slave masters as a means of honoring God's name. I propose, then, when Paul speaks of slaves honoring their masters, he does not mean unquestioned obedience. Drawing on the prophetic tradition, he has in mind behaving in such a way that their masters are drawn to God. This included, according to the Old Testament testimony, periodic refusal to obey.[45] This is not slavery as evangelism. Instead, it is saying that even in slavery one has some ability to live in a way that testifies to their beliefs.

The second scenario in 1 Timothy 6:1-3 deals with Christian masters and Christian slaves. Paul asks the slaves to treat their masters with respect. It is important to note that Paul sees the enslaved person as a moral agent and not simply a tool. He instructs them as those capable of making decisions. He also seems to suggest that there is something in the gospel that makes them look upon their masters differently. The gospel, as Paul preached it, apparently did upset dynamics. Paul does not go all the way and say, let's actualize what the gospel implies. Instead he says that even in this changed circumstance we still owe them love and respect as the church begins to fully implement the realities of the gospel. The structures remain in place here at least even if the gospel has weakened their power.

So what are we to make of this passage? I think that we should see 1 Timothy 6:1-3 in much the same way that we see the slave laws of the Old Testament. Paul is trying to make pastoral sense of a difficult

---

[45]"Look, with me here, my master has no concern about anything in the house, and he has put everything that he has in my hand. He is not greater in this house than I am, nor has he kept back anything from me except yourself, because you are his wife. How then could I do this great wickedness, and sin against God?" (Gen 39:8-9)

situation. We are not limited to his solution, but we can be inspired by his example. Paul, despite claims to the contrary, sought to limit the damage done by slavery and rethought the whole institution in light of the cross and resurrection. Nothing in Paul's imaginative world remained the same after he came to believe in the resurrection. Slavery had to change like everything else. The church should have, much sooner than it did, been able to implement more fully the implications of the gospel in the United States and beyond. We should have freed the slaves.

CONCLUSION

We began with a question posed by James Pennington. Did the God he served support slavery? He thought that all hung on that question. This a very dangerous question for the Black Christian to ask because we do not know what awaits us on the other side of asking. We began by looking at the exegetical model given to us by Christ. Jesus argues from God's wider creational purposes rather than particular passages of the Old Testament. He maintained that some passages limit human sin rather than present the ideal. Therefore, we are not limited to those passages when constructing a properly Christian theology. I argued that since slavery was not God's original intention, the Christian could reason from creation to the liberation of the enslaved. Furthermore, we could reason back from Christian eschatology to present freedom as a foretaste.

I argued that the Old and New Testaments, even the letters of Paul, provide us with the theological resources to dismantle slavery. It is simply false to claim that the Old and New Testaments simply baptize the institutions as they find them. Instead, the Scriptures raise tensions between the central themes of the Bible and slavery.

Are these hints and starts enough by themselves? A full discussion of Christianity and slavery would involve a discussion of how all its beliefs work together to end slavery including: the command to love one another, the warning against greed and sexual immorality, the atonement, the image of God, justification, and justice. *Together* these doctrines make the institution unacceptable in the long term, but rather than making that argument here, I close with the answer that Pennington came to after a life of struggle. It represents a former slave's conclusion on the matter:

> My sentence is that slavery is condemned by the general tenor and scope of the New Testament. Its doctrines, its precepts, and all its warnings against the system. I am not bound to show that the New Testament authorizes me in such a chapter and verse to reject a slaveholder. It is sufficient for me to show what is acknowledged by my opponents, that it is murdering the poor, corrupting society, alienating the brethren, and sowing the seed of discord in the bosom of the whole church. . . . Let us always bear in mind of what slavery is and what the gospel is.[46]

---

[46]Pennington, *Two Years Absence*, 27.

CONCLUSION

AN EXERCISE IN HOPE

■ ■ ■

And hope does not put us to shame, because God's love
has been poured out into our hearts through the
Holy Spirit, who has been given to us.

ROMANS 5:5 NIV

It's been a long, a long time coming,
but I know a change gon' come.

SAM COOKE

THIS BOOK BEGAN WITH A CLAIM, namely that the Black ecclesial tradition, of which I am one of many heirs, has a distinctive message of hope arising from its reading of biblical texts. This message of hope is not simply a thing of the past; it is living and active, having the ability to provide a way forward for Black believers who continue to turn to the Scriptures for guidance. On a personal level, this book was an attempt to fulfill a trust given to me by my mother and the church of my childhood. I wanted them and other Black Christians to see something of themselves on the pages. This book is not successful if it has been innovative; I have succeeded if it has reminded others of home.

I have tried to put into print a habit or an instinct that defies easy description. You capture hints of it in Black songs and prayers. You can find it in our sermons and prayer meetings that stretched long into the night. It exists around dinner tables, at gravesides, and in speeches that stirred the conscience of a nation. It includes a patience with the biblical text rooted in the confidence that God has willed our good and not our harm.

This tradition of Bible reading is canonical and theological at its core, placing its greatest hopes in the character of God as it emerges from the entirety of the biblical story. It builds on the great truths of God as creator, liberator, savior, and judge. The tradition of biblical interpretation is dialogical, clearly beginning with the concerns of Black Christians, but being willing to listen to the Scriptures as God speaks back to us. We have a patience with the biblical text born of its use against us. We have had to wrestle like Jacob until the text delivered its blessing.

I noted that some might doubt this tradition's ability to address issues facing Christians today. Therefore, I turned my eye toward some questions that seemed pressing to this writer:

- Does the Bible have a word to say about the creation of a just society in which Black people can flourish free of oppression?

- Does the Bible speak to the issue of policing—that constant source of fear in the Black community?

- Does the Bible provide us with the warrant to protest injustice when we encounter it?

- Does the Bible value our ethnic identity? Does God love our blackness?

- What shall we do about the pain and rage that comes with being Black in this country?

- What about slavery? Did the God of the Bible sanction what happened to us?

More questions could have been asked, but being exhaustive was never the aim. I wanted to continue a conversation, not conclude it. I will leave it to the reader to decide if I succeeded in answering these questions to anyone's satisfaction. But whether I accomplished that goal or failed is not the point. The point is that the very process of *engaging* these Scriptures and *expecting* an answer is an exercise in hope. It is an act of faith that has carried Black people through unimaginable despair toward a brighter future. The Bible has been a source of comfort, but it has also been more. It has inspired action to transform circumstances. It has liberated Black bodies and souls.

So what comes next? I hope that this book inspires more biblical scholarship rooted in the Black ecclesial tradition's deepest instincts and habits (if I have gotten them right). I hope that the mainline tradition, the evangelical tradition, and the Black progressive tradition have found another conversation partner that deserves respect. I also hope that I have provided a path Christians can follow to see in these texts a friend and not an enemy. But this is just a beginning.

The questions I have asked deserve much greater scrutiny. These chapters are sketches toward a much deeper and wider engagement with the Bible and the hopes of Black folks. The question of policing in the New Testament and its relationship to Black bodies in this country is a monograph begging to be written. (You had better hurry because I might write it first.) Our theology of public witness and protest in the field of biblical studies remains anemic. We have allowed a few misapplied passages to dominate the conversation for far too long. We have allowed man made (I use the term *man* intentionally) rules to create a hermeneutical prison that traps biblical scholarship in the past. It is time to let the lion out to hunt. Ethnic

identity and the Christian community, a question asked and answered a generation ago must be addressed again in our day so that
our people know that God glories in the distinctive gifts we all bring
into the kingdom. Black pain and the anger rising from it is not going
away. Therefore, the long tradition of Black reflection on our pain
will continue. The slave question will be with us until the eschaton.
Therefore we must continue to read, write, interpret, and hope until
the advent of the one who will answer all our questions, or render
them redundant.

BONUS TRACK

FURTHER NOTES ON THE DEVELOPMENT
OF BLACK ECCLESIAL INTERPRETATION

■ ■ ■

THERE HAVE BEEN MANY DETAILED ACCOUNTS of the history of
Black biblical interpretation.[1] Rather than improve on these more
extensive summaries, I will provide a brief overview of my reading
of this tradition, while highlighting some neglected pieces of evidence. My goal is to provide a historical and theological framework
for my proposals on Black ecclesial interpretation.[2]

Many recognize that Black Christianity began as a counter-interpretation. Black slaves, for the most part, first encountered
Christianity in America as an attempt to control and content them
with their fate in this world while hoping for a better future in the
next. Francis Le Jau, an Anglican missionary to South Carolina, is

---

[1]Mitzi Smith, *Insights from African American Interpretation* (Minneapolis, MN: Fortress
Press, 2017), 1-76; Allen Dwight Callahan, *The Talking Book: African Americans and the
Bible* (New Haven, CT: Yale University Press, 2006); Vincent Wimbush, "The Bible and
African Americans: An Outline of an Interpretive History," in *Stony the Road We Trod:
African American Biblical Interpretation*, ed. Cain Hope Felder (Minneapolis, MN: Augsburg Fortress, 1991), 81-97.
[2]Unfortunately, much of the period between 1920 and the beginning of Black Theology in
the 1960s will be neglected for the sake of space.

indicative of this practice. He forced the enslaved person to agree to the following before he would baptize them:

> You declare in the presence of God and before this congregation that you do not ask for Holy baptism out of any design to free yourself from the duty and obedience that you owe your master while you live, but merely for the good of your soul and to partake of the graces and blessings promised to members of the church of Jesus Christ.[3]

It is no surprise that many rejected this severely limited gospel.[4] Nonetheless, Black conversion to Christ began on a large scale during the Great Awakening of the mid-eighteenth century.[5] The revivals succeeded where the previous attempts of Anglicans and Puritans failed because they had a vigor and urgency that the more stayed traditions lacked.[6]

Alongside the vibrancy of evangelicalism, there was, in spirit if not always in practice, an emphasis on the equality of all people due to the belief that all were sinners in need of God's grace. The equal need for grace spoke to the equal worth of Black bodies and souls, making conversion to this form of Christianity a realistic possibility. Furthermore, the flexible polities of Baptist and later Methodist churches made it easier for African Americans to form their own independent churches and denominations when racism forced them out of white churches. Here in these newly formed Black churches and denominations we have our first extensive record of the Black encounter with the Bible.

---

[3]Quoted in Albert J. Raboteau, *Canaan Land: A Religious History of African Americans*, Religion in American Life (New York: Oxford University Press, 2001), 16.

[4]Allen Dwight Callahan, *The Talking Book: African Americans and the Bible* (New Haven, CT: Yale University Press, 2006), 3.

[5]Raboteau, *Canaan Land*, 16-17; H. L. Whelchel, *The History and Heritage of African-American Churches: A Way Out of No Way* (St. Paul, MN: Paragon House, 2011), 83.

[6]Whelchel, *The History and Heritage of African-American Churches*, 84.

The emphasis on the Bible in evangelical circles spurred on the Black desire for literacy. Learning to read the Bible helped expand the world and imagination of slaves, making them more difficult to control. This led to attempts to limit Bible reading among slaves out of fear it might cause rebellion.[7] Slave masters' fear of the Bible must bear some indirect testimony to what the slave masters thought it said. Part of them knew that their exegetical conclusions could only be maintained if the enslaved were denied firsthand experience of the text. This is evidence to my mind that Bible reading was itself an act against despair and for hope.

We can witness at least three responses arising from the Black encounter with the Bible in this period. Some formerly enslaved people used the Bible to argue against color-based racism and slavery, a favorite text being the rendering of Acts 17:26 in the King James Version. It said that God "hath made of one blood all nations of men for to dwell on the face of the earth."[8] According to many Black believers, this common origin ruled out race-based slavery. Others seemed to internalize at least in part the negative understanding of Black worth found among white Christians.[9] It has been common to mention Phyllis Wheatley and Jupiter Hammon in this group.[10] Hammon's "Address to the Negroes in the State of New York," is known for its call for enslaved people to accept their plight based upon the standard interpretations of Paul amongst white slave owners. Hammon's address also includes some skepticism about Black moral capabilities that can be found in the literatures of enslavers. Other scholarship

---

[7]Whelchel, *The History and Heritage of African-American Churches*, 90.

[8]See Olaudah Equiano, "Traditional Ibo Religion and Culture," in *African American Religious History: A Documentary Witness*, ed. Milton C. Sernett (Durham, NC: Duke University Press), 18.

[9]See Jupiter Hammon, "Address to the Negroes in the Sates of New York," in *African American Religious History*, 34-43.

[10]Eleanor Smith, "Phillis Wheatley: A Black Perspective," *The Journal of Negro Education* 43, no. 3 (1974): 401-7.

has questioned some of our oversimplified readings of these two.[11] Nonetheless, it is fair to say that they reflected a more muted critique of American Christianity that is somewhat understandable given their status as enslaved people. A third strand of Black interpretation contended that the Bible called for an exodus-like revolt for freedom. Nat Turner is paradigmatic of this strand of interpretation. He maintained that he was called by God to lead this rebellion, which in part sprung from his interpretation of the Bible.

Most Black writers from this period saw in the texts of the Old and New Testament a message calling for liberation from *actual* slavery. This call for the end of slavery did not mean that they neglected personal salvation from sin. This call for individual and societal transformation within the context of the historic confessions of Christianity is what I came to think of as the mainstream or at least a significant strand of the Black ecclesial tradition.

It has become common to assert that enslaved people were drawn to the Bible because of its depiction of freedom from slavery. A recourse to the primary texts will show that testimonies abound of the joy of salvation.[12] This bifocal appropriation of the Christian message as a power that can bring about personal and societal change is the Black Christian tradition's gift to the American church. These three realities (critique, acquiescence, and rebellion) sit side by side, not so much as interpretative methods, but responses to what African Americans saw in the text. One sought to end racism and form a family rooted in our mutual recognition of the *imago Dei* and belief in the lordship of Christ.[13] Another group accepted the Black plight

---

[11]On Wheatley, see Sondra O'Neale, "A Subtle War: Phyllis Wheatley's Use of Biblical Myth and Symbol," *Early American Literature* 21 (1986), 144-65, and the recently discovered poem by Hammon discussed in Cedric May and Julie McCown, "An Essay on Slavery: An Unpublished Poem by Jupiter Hammon," *Early American Literature* 40 (2013), 457-71.

[12]Whelchel, *The History and Heritage of African-American Churches*, 85.

[13]Brian K. Blount, *Then the Whisper Put on Flesh: New Testament Ethics in an African American Context* (Nashville: Abingdon Press, 2001), 26-28.

and tried to make the most of it, looking for an eschatological re-demption. A third saw hope in revolution.

THE EARLY TESTIMONY OF BLACK CHURCHES

Some scholars depict the early Black interpretive method as the fore-runner of modern interpreters who put their concerns at the forefront of biblical interpretation.[14] It is surely correct that the enslaved people brought their concerns to the text. But were the white slaveholders disinterested readers of the biblical material who happened upon an interpretation that justified their physical, psychological, and financial superiority over Africans? Slaveholders were not disinterested exe-getes. They put their lust for power and material wealth *in front of the text* and read the Bible from that perspective.

If the Black Christians weren't the first to put their concerns in front of the text, what marks them out as unique? If there is a place to find the answer to this question, it is surely in the Black churches formed around this period. They repeatedly state that they created churches to worship God faithfully. The key problem was not the doctrines of the Christian faith, but the praxis of the slave masters. The African Methodist Episcopal Church (AME) was started because the white Methodist Episcopal church re-moved Black Christians from a church during a time of prayer.[15] According to the AME, the behavior of their white counterparts was *unChristian*. Thus, they needed to form their own commu-nities so that they might practice *Christianity* properly. They used this freedom to include a strong denunciation of slavery in their book of discipline. It reads

---

[14]Blount, *Then the Whisper Put on Flesh*, 34.

[15]African Methodist Episcopal Church, *The Doctrines and Discipline of the African Meth-odist Episcopal Church* (Philadelphia: Richard Allen and Jacob Tapsico, 1817), 3.

Question. WHAT shall be done for the extermination of slavery?

Answer. We will not receive any person into our society, as a member, who is a slave-holder; and any who are now members, that have slaves, and refuse to emancipate them after notification being given by the preacher having the charge, shall be excluded.[16]

The AME located the problem in Christian practice, not the received doctrine of Scripture. We observe no adjustment in the Methodist (and behind that, Anglican) belief that the Scriptures contain all things necessary for life and salvation.[17]

The Black Baptists, whose national convention began in 1886, also sought independence because they wanted freedom to practice the Christian faith. They too saw no need to revise the essentials of the Christian faith.[18] Much like the Methodists, in addition to traditional theology, there was an emphasis on social action. William J. Simmons, the first president of the convention, describes the early Black churches in the following manner:

God has permitted us to triumph and through Him. He implanted in us a vigorous spiritual tree, and since freedom, how has this been growing? Untrammeled, we have, out of our ignorance and penury, built thousands of churches, started thousands of schools, educated millions of children, supported thousands of ministers of the Gospel, organized societies for the care of the sick and the burying of the dead. This spirituality and love of offspring are indubitable evidences that slavery, though long and protracted, met in our race a vigorous,

---

[16]African Methodist Episcopal Church, *Doctrines and Discipline*, 190.

[17]African Methodist Episcopal Church, *Doctrines and Discipline*, 13-14.

[18]C. Eric Lincoln and Lawrence H. Mamiya, *The Black Church in the African American Experience* (Durham, NC: Duke University Press, 1990), 28; Walter H. Brooks, *The Silver Bluff Church: A History of Negro Baptist Churches in America* (Washington, DC: Press of R. L. Pendleton, 1910), 11-20; See the National Baptists' current statement of belief here: www.nationalbaptist.com/about-nbc/what-we-believe.

vital, God-like spirituality, which like the palm tree flourishes and climbs upward through opposition.[19]

Here we see Simmons lauding the church's service to the community and its fidelity to the gospel in the face of opposition. A perusal of the founding of the Church of God in Christ (COGIC) would lead to much the same conclusion as it relates to orthodoxy and orthopraxy. One notable difference is that Black Pentecostals did not break from a white denomination. Instead, white pastors were initially ordained by Black pastors before breaking away to form their groups.

Together, the Methodists, Pentecostals, and the Baptists represent the earliest independent Black encounters with the Bible. They drew up statements that reflected the beliefs of their communities. If the early African American witness matters, then it is important to note that these churches did not locate the problem with the Scriptures themselves, but rather with the interpretation of these texts. Furthermore, it is incorrect to claim that these early readers were concerned with the Bible only inasmuch as it spoke directly to their liberation from social and economic oppression. These were major concerns, but we see a strong affirmation of the Bible's ability to change their spiritual conditions. They could affirm the one without denying the other.

This should not be construed as saying that there was not a great diversity of belief surrounding the Bible and its interpretation in the first century of the African American encounter with the Scriptures.[20] It is to say that elements of African American biblical interpretation, insofar as it is skeptical about the authority and worth of the Bible as a whole, is discontinuous with the majority of the earliest Black

---

[19]William J. Simmons, *Men of Mark: Eminent, Progressive and Rising* (Cleveland, OH: Geo M. Rewell & Co, 1887), 8.
[20]This is chronicled by Callahan, *Talking Book.*

readers. If we want to know how the earliest Black believers read the Bible, the answer is in the sermons, testimonies, and early confessional statements of Black Christians.

On the whole these early Black Christians combined a strong affirmation of the need for personal salvation with varying levels of social action and resistance. This is readily understandable. If the Black Churches grew out of and in dialogue with the evangelical churches of the Great Awakening, it is not surprising that they would have a great affection for the Scriptures, even when they rejected the interpretations forced on them. All Christians are a part of one story and are in varying levels of dialogue with past and present interpretations. Christian communities do not spring into existence ex nihilo. The early Black church's reorientation of the gospel to a more holistic and faithful witness than the one on offer by slaveholders is a manifestation of this ongoing conversation about the nature of the Christian faith.

BLACK THEOLOGY AND AFRICAN AMERICAN BIBLICAL INTERPRETATION

Despite the formation of Black Churches in the eighteenth century, Black academic study of the Bible did not begin in earnest until the middle of the twentieth century when Leon White became the first African American to receive a PhD in New Testament.[21] This lack of Biblical scholars was not due to a lack of interest, but rather the long history of institutional racism that limited Black access to higher education.[22]

---

[21]Michael Joseph Brown, *The Blackening of the Bible: The Aims of African American Biblical Scholarship* (Harrisburg, PA: Trinity Press International, 2004), 19. Renita Weems, some fifty years later, would become the first Black female to earn a PhD in Old Testament from an American seminary. See Brown, *Blackening of the Bible*, 93.

[22]Smith, *Insights from African American Interpretation*, 25-26.

The first generation of Black biblical scholars focused largely on correcting the Eurocentric account of biblical history that denied the Black presence in the Bible. Prominent in this group were Charles Copher and Cain Hope Felder.[23] Combining an analysis of Old Testament texts, historical evidence, and contemporary views on race, Copher contended that

> from slaves to rulers, from court officials to authors who wrote parts of the Old Testament itself, from lawgivers to prophets, black peoples and their lands and individual black persons appear numerous times. In the veins of Hebrew-Israelite-Judahite-Jewish peoples flowed black blood.[24]

The point of their work was plain enough. They wanted to make it clear that African peoples had been a part of God's redemptive purposes from the beginning.

This foundational work is not complete. Some still do not appreciate the African presence in the Bible. It remains a fact hiding in plain sight.[25] Even if we do not agree with all their conclusions, this work was vital in helping African Americans understand that they are part of the grand story of redemption.[26] The influence of their work can be seen in my reflections on the Bible and Black identity. They went beyond a recovery of Black presence; they also wanted to draw on the Liberation theologies coming of age in the sixties and seventies to inform their interpretative method.[27]

---

[23]Cain Hope Felder, *Troubling Biblical Waters: Race, Class, and Family* (Maryknoll, NY: Orbis Books, 1989); Cain Hope Felder, "Race, Racism, and the Biblical Narratives," in *Stony the Road We Trod*, 127-45; Charles B. Copher, "The Black Presence in the Old Testament," in *Stony the Road We Trod*, 146-64. See also his anthology in Charles B. Copher, *Black Biblical Studies: Biblical and Theological Issues on the Black Presence in the Bible* (Chicago: Black Light Fellowship, 1993).

[24]Copher, "Black Presence in the Old Testament," 164. For an analysis of these claims see Brown, *Blackening of the Bible*, 25-34.

[25]See my elementary discussion of Black presence in the Bible in chapter five.

[26]See the closer reading of Brown, *Blackening of the Bible*, 24-53.

[27]Felder, *Troubling Biblical Waters*, xii-xiii.

James Cone is recognized by all as a seminal figure in the creation of Black Liberation theology. No analysis of the Black ecclesial tradition could be complete without some interaction with him. This justifies a brief look at Cone's interpretative method as seen in his essay, "Biblical Revelation and Social Existence."[28] Cone rightly argues that all theology is socially located. According to Cone, this is a good thing because acknowledging social location affirms the goodness of the creation in which God has placed his people.[29] Therefore, God's choice of enslaved Israel to be his chosen people spoke to his character. Cone says, "If God had chosen as his 'holy nation' the Egyptian slave masters instead of the Israelite slaves a completely different kind of God would have been revealed. Thus, Israel's election cannot be separated from her servitude and liberation."[30] The habit of highlighting the social location of biblical characters in our own readings and applications of the Bible is an insight I carried forward in my proposal.

Cone goes on to discuss the fact that the call to covenant was an act of grace and that God's grace sustained it. During the monarchy the prophets called Israel back to covenant faithfulness in two ways: Israelites should put their trust in Yahweh alone and stop oppressing the poor. Thus, for Cone, the Old Testament reveals a God of liberation who calls his people to be faithful to him because of their liberation. The New Testament, for Cone, fulfilled the Old in that Jesus' life and ministry embodied the call for liberation and concern for the marginalized.[31] Cone, then, advocates a reading that highlights God's transformation of political systems and claims that this transformation stands at the center of the biblical message. He says,

---

[28]James H. Cone, "Biblical Revelation and Social Existence," *Interpretation* 28, no. 4 (1974): 422-40.

[29]Cone, "Biblical Revelation," 160-61.

[30]Cone, "Biblical Revelation," 162.

[31]Cone, "Biblical Revelation," 168.

The hermeneutical principle for an exegesis of the scriptures is the revelation of God in Christ as the liberator of the oppressed from social oppression and to political struggle, wherein the poor recognize that their fight against poverty and injustice is not only consistent with the gospel but is the gospel of Christ.[32]

It is the totalizing nature of this claim that gave me significant pause and seemed to separate Cone from a significant strand of the Black Christian tradition that combined the transformation of systems with the individual transformation of life. His definition of the gospel in this article appears to be at odds with the biblical narrative upon which such a claim resides.

Is it accurate to claim that political liberation is so much the overriding concern of the Old and New Testaments that we can claim that it *is the gospel of Christ*? In the biblical material, Exodus gives to Leviticus the formation of a cult and a people whose holiness of life reflected something of the nature of God. Texts such as the *Magnificat* and passages in the Psalms and prophets emphasize the upsetting of social structures, but those same biblical texts call upon the newly freed to repent of their sins and commit to the transformed lives indicative of the change brought about by the Messiah Jesus.[33]

Isaiah 5:7-8 denounced the exploitation of the poor. Then a few verses later the prophet expresses his displeasure about the personal morality of the citizens of Judah. He says, "Ah, [woe to] you who rise early in the morning / in pursuit of strong drink, / who linger in the evening / to be inflamed by wine" (Is 5:11). The prophet's message includes both the call for the end of oppression and a transformation of the character of individuals in Judah.

---

[32]Cone, "Biblical Revelation," 174.
[33]See Cone, "Biblical Revelation," 167-68, on the Magnificat.

In addition, I agreed with Cone and others' assertion that Jesus' crucifixion was an act of state-sponsored terror, and his resurrection does empty the state of its most prized weapon, the power of life and death.[34] However, the death of Christ is not merely a critique of the totalizing and oppressing power of the state. It is also, according to a variety of texts right across the New Testament, a means of reconciling God and humanity.[35] It is an act of atonement that brings about the forgiveness of sins (Rom 4:25). Therefore, it seems fair to say that Cone picks upon the liberative aspects that marked the early Black interpretation of the Bible while possibly not giving as much attention to the conversionistic and holiness strands that were equally prominent. I tried to gather all three in the exegetical chapters in this book, while making sure that the liberative stream was influenced by Jesus' own cruciform example.

The recovery of Black presence took on a slightly different form in the authors who built upon the early work on this subject.[36] First there was a shift in focus from Black presence to Black agency. It was not sufficient to note the presence of Black figures. Scholars wanted to know how these individuals functioned in the text.[37] There was also a growth in the interpretation of biblical texts from a decidedly

---

[34]James Cone, *A Black Theology of Liberation*, 40th Anniversary Edition (New York: Orbis Books, 1970), 124-25.

[35]I am not claiming that Cone denies that the cross reconciles God and humanity or that the cross brings about the forgiveness of sins. I do want to contend that it may be possible that in his attempt to address an imbalance in accounts of the cross that downplay God's identification with the oppressed, other important aspects of the cross fade from view. What we need is a creative synthesis that brings these various facets together in the same work.

[36]Smith, *Insights from African American Interpretation*, 31-48; Brown, *Blackening of the Bible*, 54-88.

[37]Randall Bailey, "Is That Any Name for a Nice Hebrew Boy?," in *The Recovery of Black Presence: An Interdisciplinary Exploration: Essays in Honor of Dr. Charles B. Copher* (Nashville: Abingdon Press, 1995), 27-54, for example, argues that Moses' mother was African and then focuses on her actions in Exodus 2:1-10.

African American perspective.[38] We also see a turn to Black primary
sources: the early preachers, teachers, evangelists, and even later
fiction writers. This corpus was originally deemed the "Black fathers,"
but today we would rightly remember them as the Black mothers
and fathers of the faith.[39]

Probably the most important recent development in African
American biblical interpretation has been the development of womanist biblical interpretation. The term *womanist* comes from Alice
Walker, who used the term to refer to a form of feminism that explicitly
links issues of race to an appreciation of the abilities of and advocacy
for the rights of Black women.[40] As it relates to biblical studies, womanism has come to refer to a form of interpretation that joins together
what many feel has been taken apart. Womanist scholars critique white
feminism for its failure to examine its own privilege and for its neglect
of issues of race. It also critiques Black theology because it focused on
racism to the exclusion of sexism and patriarchy. St. Clair, quoting
Jones-Warsaw, offers the following definition. Womanist interpretation involves, "discover[ing] the significance and validity of the biblical text for Black women who today experience the 'tridimensional
reality' of racism, sexism, and classism."[41] Womanism is not the whole

[38]Smith, *Insights from African American Interpretation*, 28, notes Blount's work on Mark.
He has also published more recently on Revelation in Blount, *Can I Get A Witness? Read-
ing Revelation Through African American Culture* (Louisville, KY: Westminster John
Knox Press, 2005). See also Brad Braxton, *No Longer Slaves: Galatians and African
American Experience* (Collegeville, MN: The Liturgical Press, 2002), and Brian K. Blount,
True to Our Native Land: An African American New Testament Commentary
(Minneapolis, MN: Fortress Press, 2007).

[39]Frederick L. Ware, *Methodologies of Black Theology* (Eugene, OR: Wipf and Stock, 2002),
28; See also Smith, *Insights from African American Interpretation*, 51; Vincent Wimbush,
"Introduction: Reading Darkness, Reading Scriptures," in *African Americans and the
Bible: Sacred Texts and Social Textures*, ed. Vincent Wimbush (New York: Continuum,
2001), 1-49.

[40]See Nyasha Junior, *An Introduction to Womanist Biblical Interpretation* (Louisville, KY:
Westminster John Knox Press, 2015), xi-xxv, for an extended discussion of the ways that
the appropriation of Walker differed from her intent.

[41]Raquel St. Clair, "Womanist Biblical Interpretation," in *True to Our Native Land*, 54.

of the Black female exegetical enterprise.[42] Some Black women identify as womanist, and some do not.[43] By whatever name they go, the voices of black women are vital if the whole people of God are to join in the interpretative process.

In addition to the rise of womanism and the focus on agency, recent trends have included problematization of the biblical text. Smith says, "African American biblical scholars increasingly acknowledge and 'address the elephant in the room'... affirming what many of our African Ancestors previously contended: sometimes there's a problem with the biblical (con)text itself. The biblical text is not synonymous with God."[44] Smith is correct that there is a long tradition of African American criticism of the Bible. But it is also fair to say that the majority of African American Christians have found ways to affirm some ongoing normative role of the Old and New Testaments. Many black interpreters did what Bible readers throughout time have done, engaged in a canonical reading of the text that questions overly reductionistic interpretations and applications. This should not be heard as a dismissal of the valid concerns like the questions womanist scholars have raised about the imagery and depiction of women in biblical texts.[45] Nor does it mean that we can wave our hand at the canon and dismiss the difficulties in the Bible. The job of the scholar is to probe and press and challenge simplistic readings. It is also important to challenge simplistic readings using our own experiences that might provide insights that others who do not share those experiences might have missed.

---

[42]See Nyasha Junior, *An Introduction to Womanist Biblical Interpretation* (Louisville, KY: Westminster John Knox Press, 2015).

[43]See Cheryl J. Sanders, Cheryl Townsend Gilkes, Katie G. Cannon, Emilie M. Townes, M. Shawn Copeland, and Bell Hooks, "Roundtable Discussion: Christian Ethics and Theology in Womanist Perspective," *Journal of Feminist Studies in Religion* 5, no. 2 (1989): 83-112.

[44]Smith, *Insights from African American Interpretation*, 66.

[45]See Renita Weems, *Battered Love: Marriage, Sex, and Violence in the Hebrew Prophets* (Minneapolis, MN: Fortress Press, 1995).

Nonetheless, and here I speak to interpreters generally, there is a difference between acknowledging the social location of interpretation and letting said location eclipse the text itself. There must be places where the Bible actually *shapes* Black Christian thought by telling us things that we did not already know. The only way that it can speak to us is if we acknowledge in some sense its own self-presentation as a place of meeting between God and humanity. In other words, there must be more to the Black interpretative method than affirming the desire for political liberation, the terms of which are largely decided apart from a serious engagement with the biblical text. Brown notices this trend of rejecting the normative role of the Bible when he says, "A great deal of African American biblical hermeneutics is a reaction or response to the perceived advancement of evangelical Christianity and fundamentalism in the African American community."[46]

It is here, in its critique of the traditional beliefs of the African American community, that elements of Black progressive tradition reveal its dependency on its *origins*. If we can affirm the fact that early Black traditionalists were influenced by their evangelical roots, we can also acknowledge the dependency of the early tradition of Black theology on the progressive turn in mainline seminaries, denominations, and universities.[47] Black progressivism, like Black traditionalism, did not spring into existence ex nihilo. In some ways, the tension between the Black church in the pews and the Black academy reflects a parallel conversation going on between white evangelicals and white progressives.[48] The unfortunate thing is that in the Black community there should be more room for cooperation

---

[46]Brown, *Blackening the Bible*, 154-55.

[47]Brown, *Blackening the Bible*, 154, notes that liberation theology is a response to modernity and that Black theology is a part of this enterprise.

[48]Smith, *Insights from African American Interpretation*, 23-24; and Brown, *Blackening the Bible*, 23, note the tension between academic and popular Black theology.

since both sides often agree on many issues related to Christianity and justice for the disinherited. We also do not have the experience of creating separate institutions or churches. Black progressives and Black traditionalists live, work, and go to church together.

Based on my readings of this tradition outlined above, I noticed a few things. First, there is no one Black tradition, but at least three streams: revolutionary/nationalistic, reformist/transformist, and conformist.[49] Much of the modern academic dialogue highlights the heirs to the revolutionary and conformist tradition. I hoped to make a case for a third thing within the African American tradition. Second, I noticed that there were some common tendencies among the reformist/transformist stream. I named this the Black ecclesial tradition because I think it lives on in pulpits even if it is less often in print.

I suggested that Black ecclesial interpretation is clearly *socially located*. It attempts to make sense of what it means to be Black and Christian. When I said it is *theological* I meant that it uses theological concepts like the character of God or the *imago Dei* to argue that the interpretive method used to justify slavery had to be wrong because it violated what could be known of God's character. This led to a third point, namely that the Black interpretative tradition was *canonical*. When faced with difficult passages like 1 Timothy 6:1-3, they turned to the wider testimony of the Scriptures and read individual texts in light of the whole biblical narrative. The method also displayed *patience*, because the initial instinct might be to reject the Bible as an authority due to their negative experience of it. They did not. Because of the legacy of enslavers using the Bible to oppress Black people, there is a long history of Black secular criticism of

---

[49]For example, I would locate James Cone within the revolutionary stream. I might place J. Doetis Roberts in the transformist or revolutionary stream. Few would want to self-identify as conformist.

Christianity. Black believers therefore have had to develop a *double apologetic*, answering questions posed by Black secularists *and* white progressives. These tools, if I have read the tradition correctly, allowed early Black believers to argue that there was a difference between true Christianity and its distortion. The habit of using these tools in their interpretation of the Bible to discern the truth of the Christian faith from its opposite is what I am calling *Black ecclesial interpretation*. If this work has gone some way toward helping another generation make the same distinctions, then it has done its job.

DISCUSSION GUIDE

■ ■ ■

1. In chapter one, I discuss the limits of the different interpretative communities that I have known. How has the community in which you were raised both helped and hindered your interpretation of the Bible?

2. I claim that the black ecclesial interpretation lives largely in the pulpits of Black churches and rarely in print. What is your experience with Black churches? Does my description of them match your experience? If you have never spent time attending Black churches, why not?

3. Chapter two makes a biblical case for police reform. Are there other examples of policing in the Old or New Testament that might strengthen my case? What do you make of the examples that I cite? Why does an issue that seems so important to African Americans see so little theological or exegetical reflection?

4. Chapter three covers the political witness of the church. What is your church's stance on political advocacy? If my exegetical argument is sound, how might that impact the way in which your church engages in advocacy for the disinherited? What other

interactions between Old and New Testament leaders and government officials might be added to what is listed there?

5. Chapter four addresses the question of justice. How have you overcome cynicism in the fight for justice? How does the witness of Black Christianity challenge our cynicism? Does Luke indeed give us all the resources to speak about the creation of a just society? What other passages in the Old and New Testament point toward the pursuit of justice?

6. Chapter five addresses the question of identity. Have you ever studied the African presence in the Bible? How has the multiethnic vision of the Bible shaped your church context? What does it mean for each culture to offer its distinctive gifts to God?

7. Chapter six addresses Black anger. Have you ever been angry or disappointed with the church? What kind of resources have you turned to? How do the Psalms of lament, the cross, and the final judgment transform our anger? Are you impressed by the fact that ancient Israel could look for more than revenge?

8. Chapter seven focuses on slavery. What do you find helpful about the method outlined here? How do we make sense of the fact that Christian support of slavery is a dark era in our history?

9. The bonus track is a more detailed review of the Black exegetical tradition. What did you learn that you didn't already know?

BIBLIOGRAPHY

African Methodist Episcopal Church. *The Doctrines and Discipline of the African Methodist Episcopal Church*. Philadelphia, PA: Richard Allen and Jacob Tapsico, 1817.

Albert, Octavia V. Rogers. *The House of Bondage*. New York: Hunt and Eaton, 1890.

Allison, Dale C. *The New Moses: A Matthean Typology*. Minneapolis, MN: Fortress, 1999.

Anderson, Bernhard W. *Out of the Depths: The Psalms Speak for Us Today*. Louisville, KY: Westminster John Knox Press, 2000.

Augustus. *Res Gestae*. Translated by Thomas Bushnell. 1998. http://classics.mit.edu/Augustus /deeds.html.

Aune, David E. *Revelation 17–22*. WBC 52C. Grand Rapids, MI: Zondervan, 1998.

Azurara, Gomes Eanes de. *The Chronicle of Discovery and Conquest of Guinea*. 2 vols. London: Hakluyt Society, 1896–1899.

Bailey, Randall. "Is That Any Name for a Nice Hebrew Boy?" In *The Recovery of Black Presence: An Interdisciplinary Exploration: Essays in Honor of Dr. Charles B. Copher*, edited by Randall C. Bailey, 27-54. Nashville: Abingdon Press, 1995.

Bartchy, S. S. "Slavery." In *The International Standard Bible Encyclopedia (Revised)*, edited by Geoffery W. Bromiley, 539-46. Accordance electronic edition, version 1.2. Grand Rapids, MI: Eerdmans, 1979.

Bass, Jonathan S. *Blessed Are the Peacemakers: Martin Luther King, Jr., Eight White Religious Leaders, and the "Letter from Birmingham Jail."* Baton Rouge, LA: LSU Press, 2001.

Bauckham, Richard. *Jesus and the Eyewitnesses: The Gospels as Eyewitness Testimony*. Grand Rapids, MI: Eerdmans, 2006.

Bebbington, David W. *Evangelicalism in Modern Britain: A History from the 1730s to the 1980s*. London: Routledge, 1989.

Blount, Brian K. *Can I Get a Witness? Reading Revelation Through African American Culture*. Louisville, KY: Westminster John Knox Press, 2005.

———. *Then the Whisper Put on Flesh: New Testament Ethics in an African American Context*. Nashville: Abingdon Press, 2001.

———. *True to Our Native Land: An African American New Testament Commentary*. Minneapolis, MN: Fortress Press, 2007.

Boring, Eugune M. "The Gospel of Matthew." In *General Articles on the New Testament: Matthew–Mark*, 90-509. NIB 8. Nashville: Abingdon Press, 1995.

Bosworth, A. B. "Vespasian and the Slave Trade." *The Classical Quarterly* 52, no. 1 (2002): 350-57.

Bovon, François. *Luke 1: A Commentary on the Gospel of Luke 1:1-9:50*. Hermeneia 63A. Edited by Helmut Koester. Translated by Christine M. Thomas. Minneapolis, MN: Fortress Press, 2002.

Braxton, Brad Ronnell. *No Longer Slaves: Galatians and African American Experience*. Collegeville, MN: Liturgical Press, 2002.

Brooks, Walter H. *The Silver Bluff Church: A History of Negro Baptist Churches in America*. Washington, DC: Press of R. L. Pendleton, 1910.

Brown, Michael Joseph. *The Blackening of the Bible: The Aims of African American Biblical Scholarship*. Harrisburg, PA: Trinity Press International, 2004.

Brown, Raymond. *An Introduction to the New Testament*. Anchor Bible Reference Library. New Haven, CT: Yale University Press, 1997.

Bruce, F. F. *The Epistles to the Colossians, to Philemon, and to the Ephesians*. NICNT. Grand Rapids, MI: Eerdmans, 1984.

Burnett, Clint. "Eschatological Prophet of Restoration: Luke's Theological Portrait of John the Baptist in Luke 3:1-6." *Neotestamentica* 47 (2013): 1-24.

Burridge, Richard. *Imitating Jesus: An Inclusive Approach to New Testament Ethics*. Grand Rapids, MI: Eerdmans, 2007.

Buth, Randall. "That Small-Fry Herod Antipas, or When a Fox Is Not a Fox." *Jerusalem Perspective*. September 1, 1993. www.jerusalemperspective.com/2667/.

Callahan, Allen Dwight. "Paul's Epistle to Philemon: Toward an Alternative Argumentum." *Harvard Theological Review* 86, no. 4 (1993): 357-76.

———. *The Talking Book: African Americans and the Bible*. New Haven, CT: Yale University Press, 2006.

Carpenter, C. C. J., et al. "A Call for Unity." April 12, 1963. www3.dbu.edu/mitchell/documents/ACallforUnityTextandBackground.pdf.

Cassidy, Ron. "The Politicization of Paul: Romans 13:1-7 in Recent Discussion." *The Expository Times* 121, no. 8 (2010): 383-89.

Christensen, Duane L. *Deuteronomy 21:10–34:12*. WBC 6B. Grand Rapids, MI: Zondervan, 2002.

Ciampa, Roy E., and Brian S. Rosner. *The First Letter to the Corinthians*. PNTC. Grand Rapids, MI: Eerdmans, 2010.

Clements, Ronald E. "The Book of Deuteronomy." In *Numbers–2 Samuel*, 271-539. NIB 2. Nashville: Abingdon Press, 1998.

Cone, James. "Biblical Revelation and Social Existence." *Interpretation* 28, no. 4 (1974): 422-40.

———. *A Black Theology of Liberation Fortieth Anniversary Edition*. New York: Orbis Books, 1970.

———. *The Cross and the Lynching Tree*. Maryknoll, NY: Orbis, 2013.

Copher, Charles B. *Black Biblical Studies: Biblical and Theological Issues on the Black Presence in the Bible*. Chicago: Black Light Fellowship, 1993.

Craigie, Peter C. *The Book of Deuteronomy*. NICOT. Grand Rapids, MI: Eerdmans, 1976.

Crowder, Stephanie Buckhanon. "Luke." In *True to Our Native Land: An African American New Testament Commentary*, edited by Brian K. Blount, 186-213. Minneapolis, MN: Fortress Press, 2007.

Culpepper, Alan R. "The Gospel of Luke." In *The Gospel of Luke–The Gospel of John*, 3-492. *NIB* 9. Nashville: Abingdon Press, 1995.

Deming, Will. "A Diatribe Pattern in 1 Cor. 7:21-22: A New Perspective on Paul's Directions to Slaves." *Novum Testamentum* 37, no. 2 (1995): 130-37.

Douglass, Frederick. *The Life of an American Slave*. Boston: Anti-Slavery Office, 1845.

———. "The Meaning of July Fourth for the Negro." July 5, 1852. http://mass humanities.org/files/programs/douglass/speech_complete.pdf.

Du Bois, W. E. B. *The Souls of Black Folk*. 1903. Reprint, New York: Dover Publications, 1994.

Dunbar, Paul Laurence. "We Wear the Mask." *Lyrics of Lowly Life*. New York: Dodd, Mead, and Company, 1896.

Dunn, James D. G. "The Letters to Timothy and the Letter to Titus." In *2 Corinthians–Philemon*, 775-882. NIB 11. Nashville: Abingdon Press, 2000.

Equiano, Olaudah. "Traditional Ibo Religion and Culture." In *African American Religious History: A Documentary Witness*, edited by Milton C. Sernett, 13-19. Durham, NC: Duke University Press, 1999.

Felder, Cain Hope. "The Letter to Philemon." In *2 Corinthians–Philemon*, 883-909. *NIB* 11. Nashville: Abingdon Press, 2000.

———. "Race, Racism, and the Biblical Narratives." In *Stony the Road We Trod: African American Biblical Interpretation*, edited by Cain Hope Felder, 127-45. Minneapolis, MN: Fortress Press, 1991.

———. *Stony the Road We Trod: African American Biblical Interpretation*. Minneapolis, MN: Fortress Press, 1991.

———. *Troubling Biblical Waters: Race, Class, and Family*. Maryknoll, NY: Orbis Books, 1989.

Fletcher-Louis, C. "Priests and Priesthood." In *Dictionary of Jesus and the Gospels*, 2nd ed., edited by Joel B. Green, Jeannine K. Brown, and Nicholas Perrin, 696-705. Downers Grove, IL: InterVarsity Press, 2013.

Flexsenhar, Michael. "Recovering Paul's Hypothetical Slaves: Rhetoric and Reality in 1 Corinthians 7:21." *Journal for the Study of Paul and His Letters* 5, no. 1 (2015): 71-88.

Fowl, Stephen. *Ephesians: A Commentary*. Louisville, KY: Westminster John Knox Press, 2012.

France, R. T. *The Gospel of Matthew*. NICNT. Grand Rapids, MI: Eerdmans, 2007.

Fuhrmann, Christopher J. *Policing the Roman Empire: Soldiers, Administration, and Public Order*. Oxford, UK: Oxford University Press, 2012.

Garland, David E. *1 Corinthians*. BECNT. Grand Rapids, MI: Baker Academic, 2003.

Gaventa, Beverly Roberts. "Is Galatians Just A 'Guy Thing'?" *Interpretation: A Journal of Bible and Theology* 54, no. 3 (2000): 267-78.

———. "Reading Romans 13 with Simone Weil: Toward a More Generous Hermeneutic." *Journal of Biblical Literature* 136, no. 1 (2017): 7.

Glancy, Jennifer A. "The Utility of an Apostle: On Philemon 11." *Journal of Early Christian History* 5, no. 1 (2015): 72-86.

González, Justo L. *Mañana: Christian Theology from a Hispanic Perspective*. Nashville: Abingdon Press, 1990.

Green, Joel. *The Gospel of Luke*. NICNT. Grand Rapids, MI: Eerdmans, 1997.

Haas, G. H. "Slave, Slavery." In *Dictionary of Old Testament: Pentateuch*, edited by T. Desmond Alexander and David W. Baker, 778-82. Downers Grove, IL: InterVarsity Press, 2003.

Häkkinen, Sakari. "Poverty in the First-Century Galilee." *Hervormde Teologiese Studies* 72, no. 4 (2016): 1-9.

Hall, Stuart G., ed. *Gregory of Nyssa, Homilies on Ecclesiastes*. Berlin: De Gruyter, 2012.

Hamilton, Victor P. *Exodus: An Exegetical Commentary*. Grand Rapids, MI: Baker Academic, 2011.

———. *The Book of Genesis: Chapters 1–17*. NICOT. Grand Rapids, MI: Eerdmans, 1990.

Harrill, J. Albert. "The Vice of Slave Dealers in Greco-Roman Society: The Use of a Topos in 1 Timothy 1:10." *Journal of Biblical Literature* 118, no. 1 (1999): 97-122.

Hays, Richard. *The Moral Vision of the New Testament: A Contemporary Introduction to New Testament Ethics*. San Francisco: HarperSanFrancisco, 1996.

Hoehner, H.W. "Herod." In *The International Standard Bible Encyclopedia (Revised)*, edited by Geoffery W. Bromiley, 588-98. Grand Rapids, MI: Eerdmans, 1979.

Holland, Tom. *Dominion: How the Christian Revolution Remade the World*. New York: Basic Books, 2019.

Horsley, Richard A. *Paul and Politics: Ekklesia, Israel, Imperium, Interpretation*. Harrisburg, PA: Trinity Press International, 2000.

Hossfeld, Frank-Lothar, and Erich Zenger. *Psalms 3: A Commentary on Psalms 101–150*. Edited by Klaus Baltzer. Translated by Linda M. Maloney. Hermeneia 19C. Minneapolis, MN: Fortress Press, 2011.

Hoyt, Thomas Jr. "Interpreting Biblical Scholarship for the Black Church Tradition." In *The Stony Road We Trod: African American Biblical Interpretation*, edited by Cain Hope Felder, 17-39. Minneapolis, MN: Fortress Press, 1991.

Ingraham, Christopher. "You Really Can Get Pulled Over for Driving While Black, Federal Statistics Show." *The Washington Post*. September 9, 2014. www.washingtonpost.com /news/wonk/wp/2014/09/09/you-really-can-get-pulled-over-for-driving-while-black -federal-statistics-show.

Isichei, Elizabeth. *A History of Christianity in Africa: From Antiquity to the Present*. London: SPCK, 1995.

Jennings, William James. *The Christian Imagination: Theology and the Origins of Race*. New Haven, CT: Yale University Press, 2010.

Jensen, Morten Hørning. "Antipas: The Herod Jesus Knew." *Biblical Archaeology Review* 38, no. 5 (September 2012): 42-46.

———. *Herod Antipas in Galilee: The Literary and Archaeological Sources on the Reign of Herod Antipas and Its Socio-Economic Impact on Galilee*. WUNT2/215. Tübingen, Germany: Mohr Siebeck, 2006.

Jewett, Robert. *Romans: A Commentary*. Minneapolis, MN: Fortress, 2007.

Johnson, Luke Timothy. *The Gospel of Luke*, Sacra Pagina. Collegeville, MN: Liturgical Press, 1991.

Johnson, M. V., J. A. Noel, and D. K. Williams, eds. *Onesimus Our Brother: Reading Religion, Race, and Culture in Philemon*. Minneapolis, MN: Fortress, 2012.

Junior, Nyasha. *An Introduction to Womanist Biblical Interpretation*. Louisville, KY: Westminster John Knox Press, 2015.

Keck, Leander. *Romans*. Abingdon New Testament Commentaries. Nashville: Abingdon Press, 2005.

Keener, Craig S. *Galatians: A Commentary.* Grand Rapids, MI: Baker Academic, 2019.

Kendi, Ibram X. *Stamped from the Beginning: The Definitive History of Racist Ideas in America.* New York: Nation Books, 2017.

King, Martin Luther, Jr. "I Have a Dream." In *I Have a Dream: Speeches and Writings that Changed the World,* edited by James M. Washington, 101-6. New York: HarperCollins, 1992.

———. "Letter from a Birmingham Jail." In *I Have a Dream: Speeches and Writings That Changed the World,* edited by James M. Washington, 83-106. New York: HarperCollins, 1992.

———. "Where Do We Go from Here?" In *I Have a Dream: Speeches and Writings That Changed the World,* edited by James M. Washington, 169-79. New York: HarperCollins, 1992.

Knight, George W., III, *The Pastoral Epistles.* NIGTC. Grand Rapids, MI: Eerdmans, 1992.

Lewis, Lloyd A. "Philemon." In *True to Our Native Land: An African American Commentary on the New Testament,* edited by Brian K. Blount, 437-43. Minneapolis, MN: Fortress Press, 2007.

Lincoln, Eric C., and Lawrence H. Mamiya. *The Black Church in the African American Experience.* Durham, NC: Duke University Press, 1990.

Lohse, Eduard. *Colossians and Philemon: A Commentary on the Epistles to the Colossians and to Philemon.* Edited by Köster Helmut. Translated by William R. Poehlmann. Minneapolis, MN: Fortress Press, 1971.

Luz, Ulrich. *Matthew 1–7: A Commentary on Matthew 1–7.* Edited by Helmut Koester. Translated by James E. Crouch. Hermeneia 61A. Minneapolis, MN: Fortress Press, 2007.

Marcus, Joel. "Herod Antipas." In *John the Baptist in History and Theology,* 98-112. Columbia, SC: University of South Carolina Press, 2018.

———. *Mark 1–8: A New Translation with Introduction and Commentary.* Anchor Bible. New York: Doubleday, 2000.

Marshall, I. Howard. *The Gospel of Luke: A Commentary on the Greek Text.* NIGTC. Grand Rapids, MI: Eerdmans, 1978.

Martin, Clarice J. "1–2 Timothy, Titus." In *True to Our Native Land: An African American Commentary on the New Testament,* edited by Brian K. Blount, 409-36. Grand Rapids, MI: Fortress Press, 2007.

Martinsen, Anders. "Was There New Life for the Social Dead in Early Christian Communities? An Ideological-Critical Interpretation of Slavery in the Household Codes." *Journal of Early Christian History* 2, no. 1 (2012): 55-69.

Martyn, James Louis. *Galatians: A New Translation with Introduction and Commentary.* Anchor Bible. New Haven, CT: Yale University Press, 1997.

May, Cedric, and Julie McCown. "An Essay on Slavery: An Unpublished Poem by Jupiter Hammon." *Early American Literature* 40 (2013), 457-71.

McCaulley, Esau. *Sharing in the Son's Inheritance: Davidic Messianism and Paul's Worldwide Interpretation of the Abrahamic Land Promise in Galatians.* London: T&T Clark, 2019.

"Members of the Historically Black Protestant Tradition Who Identify as Black." *Pew Research Forum.* www.pewforum.org/religious-landscape-study/racial-and-ethnic-composition /black/religious-tradition/historically-black-protestant.

Milgrom, Jacob. *Leviticus 23–27*. Anchor Bible. New York: Doubleday, 2001.

Mitchell, Margaret M. "John Chrysostom on Philemon: A Second Look." *Harvard Theological Review* 88, no. 1 (1995): 135-48.

Morris, Leon. *The Epistle to the Romans*. Grand Rapids, MI: Eerdmans, 1987.

———. *The Gospel According to Matthew*. PNTC. Grand Rapids, MI: Eerdmans, 1992.

Morrison, Craig E. *2 Samuel*. Berit Olam. Collegeville, MN: The Liturgical Press, 2013.

Motyer, J. Alec. *The Prophecy of Isaiah: An Introduction and Commentary*. Downers Grove, IL: InterVarsity Press, 1993.

Mounce, Robert. *The Book of Revelation*. NICNT Revised. Grand Rapids, MI: Eerdmans, 1997.

Murphy, Larry G. "Evil and Sin in African American Theology." In *The Oxford Handbook of African American Theology*, edited by Katie G. Cannon and Anthony B. Pinn, 212-27. Oxford, UK: Oxford University Press, 2014.

Noel, James A. "Nat Is Back: The Return of the Re/Oppressed in Philemon." In *Onesimus Our Brother: Reading Religion, Race, and Culture in Philemon*, edited by Matthew V. Johnson, James A. Noel, and Demetrius K. Williams, 59-90. Minneapolis, MN: Fortress Press, 2012.

Noll, Mark. *The Rise of Evangelicalism*. Downers Grove, IL: IVP Academic, 2003.

Nolland, John. *Luke 1–9:20*. WBC 35A. Grand Rapids, MI: Zondervan, 1989.

Novenson, Matthew V. *The Grammar of Messianism: An Ancient Jewish Political Idiom and Its Users*. Oxford, UK: Oxford University Press, 2017.

Oliver, Isaac W. *Torah Praxis After 70 CE: Pleading Matthew and Luke–Acts as Jewish Texts*. WUNT 2/355. Tübingen, Germany: Mohr Siebeck, 2013.

O'Neal, Sondra. "A Subtle War: Phyllis Wheatley's Use of Biblical Myth and Symbol." *Early American Literature* 21 (1986), 144-65.

Pao, David W. *Colossians and Philemon*. ZECNT. Grand Rapids, MI: Zondervan, 2012.

Parson, Michael C. *Acts*. Paideia. Grand Rapids, MI: Baker, 2008.

Payne, Daniel Alexander. "Welcome to the Ransomed." In *African American Religious History: A Documentary Witness*, edited by Milton C. Sernett, 232-44. Durham, NC: Duke University Press.

Perkins, Pheme. "Taxes in the New Testament." *The Journal of Religious Ethics* 12 (1984): 182-200.

Powery, Luke. "Gospel of Mark," In *True to Our Native Land: An African American New Testament Commentary*, edited by Brian K. Blount, 1. Minneapolis, MN: Fortress Press, 2007.

Prewitt, J. F. "Candace." In *International Standard Bible Encyclopedia (Revised)*, edited by Geoffery W. Bromiley, 591. Accordance electronic edition, version 1.2. Grand Rapids, MI: Eerdmans, 1979.

Propp, William H. C. *Exodus 19–40: A New Translation with Introduction and Commentary*. Anchor Bible. New York: Doubleday, 2006.

Raboteau, Albert J. *Canaan Land: A Religious History of African Americans*. Religion in American Life. New York: Oxford University Press, 2001.

Riesner, R. "Archeology and Geography." In *Dictionary of Jesus and the Gospels*, 2nd ed., edited by Joel B. Green, Jeannine K. Brown, and Nicholas Perrin, 45-59. Downers Grove, IL: InterVarsity Press, 2013.

Rooker, Mark F. *Leviticus*. Edited by E. Ray Clendenen and Kenneth A. Mathew. NAC 3A. Nashville: Broadman & Holman Publishers, 2000.

Rowe, C. Kavin. *Early Narrative Christology: The Lord in the Gospel of Luke*. Berlin: Walter de Gruyter, 2006.

Rowland, Christopher C. "The Book of Revelation," In *Hebrews–Revelation*, 502-745. Nashville: Abingdon Press, 1998.

Sanders, Cheryl J., Cheryl Townsend Gilkes, Katie G. Cannon, Emilie M. Townes, M. Shawn Copeland, and Bell Hooks. "Roundtable Discussion: Christian Ethics and Theology in Womanist Perspective." *Journal of Feminist Studies in Religion* 5, no. 2 (1989): 83-112.

Sarna, Nahum M. *Exodus*. The JPS Torah Commentary. Philadelphia: The Jewish Publication Society, 1991.

Sernett, Milton C., ed. *African American Religious History: A Documentary Witness*. Durham, NC: Duke University Press, 1999.

Shore, Mary Hinkle. "The Freedom of Three Christians: Paul's Letter to Philemon and the Beginning of a New Age." *Word & World* 38 (2018): 390-97.

Simmons, Martha J., and Frank A. Thomas. *Preaching with Sacred Fire: An Anthology of African American Sermons, 1750 to the Present*. New York: W. W. Norton, 2010.

Simmons, William J. *Men of Mark: Eminent, Progressive and Rising*. Cleveland, OH: Geo M. Rewell & Co, 1887.

Smith, Eleanor. "Phillis Wheatley: A Black Perspective." *The Journal of Negro Education* 43, no. 3 (1974): 401-7.

Smith, Mitzi J. *Insights from African American Interpretation*. Minneapolis, MN: Fortress Press, 2017.

———. "Utility, Fraternity, and Reconciliation: Ancient Slavery as a Context for the Return of Onesimus." In *Onesimus Our Brother: Reading Religion, Race, and Culture in Philemon*, edited by M. V. Johnson, J. A. Noel, and D. K. Williams, 47-58. Minneapolis, MN: Fortress, 2012.

Southern, Pat. *The Roman Army: A Social and Institutional History*. Santa Barbara, CA: ABC-CLIO, 2006.

Stein, Robert H. *Luke*. Edited by E. Ray Clendenen and David S. Dockery. NAC 24. Nashville: Broadman & Holman, 1992.

Stott, John. *Message of the Sermon on the Mount*. Downers Grove, IL: InterVarsity Press, 1978.

Strelan, Rick. *Luke the Priest: The Authority of the Author of the Third Gospel*. New York: Routledge, 2016.

Stuart, Douglas K. *Exodus*. NAC. Nashville: Broadman & Holman, 2006.

Stubbs, Monya A. "Subjection, Reflection, Resistance: An African American Reading of the Three-Dimensional Process of Empowerment in Romans 13 and the Free-Market." In *Navigating Romans Through Cultures: Challenging Readings by Charting a New Course*, edited by K. K. Yeo, 171-98. New York: T&T Clark, 2004.

Talbert, Charles H. *Ephesians and Colossians. Paideia Commentaries on the New Testament*. Grand Rapids, MI: Baker Academic, 2007.

Thiselton, Anthony C. *The First Epistle to the Corinthians: A Commentary on the Greek Text*. NIGTC. Grand Rapids, MI: Eerdmans, 2000.

Thurman, Howard. *Jesus and the Disinherited*. Boston: Beacon Press, 1976.

Tiroyabone, Obusitswe Kingsley. "Reading Philemon with Onesimus in the Postcolony: Exploring a Postcolonial Runaway Slave Hypothesis." *Acta Theologica* 24 (2016): 225-36.

Towner, Philip H. *The Letters to Timothy and Titus*. NICNT. Grand Rapids, MI: Eerdmans, 2006.

Ware, Frederick L. *Methodologies of Black Theology*. Eugene, OR: Wipf and Stock, 2002.

Watts, John. *Isaiah 34-66*. Grand Rapids, MI: Zondervan, 2005.

Webb, William. *Slaves, Women, and Homosexuals*. Downers Grove, IL: IVP Academic, 2001.

Weems, Renita. *Battered Love: Marriage, Sex, and Violence in the Hebrew Prophets*. Minneapolis, MN: Fortress Press, 1995.

———. "The Song of Songs." In *Introduction to Wisdom Literature: Proverbs–Sirach*, 363-436. NIB 5. Nashville: Abingdon Press, 1997.

Whelchel, H. L. *The History and Heritage of African-American Churches: A Way Out of No Way*. St. Paul, MN: Paragon House, 2011.

Wimbush, Vincent. "The Bible and African Americans: An Outline of an Interpretive History." In *Stony the Road We Trod: African American Biblical Interpretation*, edited by Cain Hope Felder, 91-97. Minneapolis, MN: Augsburg Fortress, 1991.

Wimbush, Vincent. "Introduction: Reading Darkness, Reading Scriptures." In *African Americans and the Bible: Sacred Texts and Social Textures*, edited by Vincent Wimbush, 1-49. New York: Continuum, 2001.

Wright, N. T. *Paul and the Faithfulness of God*. Minneapolis, MN: Fortress Press, 2013.

AUTHOR INDEX

Albert, Octavia V. Rogers, 144

Allen, Richard, 75, 173

Allison, Dale, 64

Anderson, Bernhard, 122

Andre3000, 1, 4

Athanasius of Alexandria, 98

Augustine of Hippo, 97

Augustus, Caesar, 37, 54

Aune, David, 63

Azurara, Gomez Eanes de, 124

Bailey, Randall, 180

Baldwin, James, 118, 120

Bartchy, S. S., 145

Bass, S. Jonathan, 48

Bauckham, Richard, 108

Bebbington, David, 10

Beverage, Albert, 146

Black, Ernest, 137

Blount, Brian, 20, 62, 64, 172, 173, 180

Boring, M. Eugene, 66

Bosworth, A. B., 53

Bovon, François, 43, 75

Braxton, Brad Ronnell, 60, 180

Brooks, Walter, 174

Brown, James, 96, 119

Brown, Michael Joseph, 176, 177, 180, 183, 183, 183

Brown, Raymond, 155

Bruce, F. F., 154

Burnett, Clint, 42

Burridge, Richard, 28

Buster, Aubrey, 151

Buth, R., 56

Caesar, Shirley, 2

Callahan, Allen Dwight, 78, 138, 153, 157, 169, 170, 175

Cannon, Katie, 146, 182

Carpenter, C. C. J., 48

Cassidy, R., 30

Christensen, Duane L., 149

Ciampa, Roy, 158

Clements, Ronald E., 149

Cleveland, James, 2

Cone, James, 138, 178-180, 184

Cooke, Sam, 164

Copeland, M. Shawn, 182

Copher, Charles, 177

Craigie, Peter, 146

Crowder, Stephanie, 76

Culpepper, R. Alan, 43, 56, 57, 75, 91

Deming, Will, 158

Douglass, Frederick, 16, 49-50, 57, 81, 126

Du Bois, W. E. B., 119

Dunbar, Paul Laurence, 125

Dunn, James D. G., 52

Equiano, Olaudah, 171

Felder, Cain Hope, 39, 155, 169, 177

Fletcher-Louis, C., 79

Flexsenhar, Michael, 158

Fowl, Stephen, 59

France, R. T., 68

Franklin, Kirk, 71

Frumentius of Axum, 98

Fuhrmann, Christopher, 29, 34-38

Garland, David E., 158

Gaventa, Beverly Roberts, 32, 61

Gilkes, Cheryl Townsend, 182

Glancy, Jennifer A., 153

Goldenberg, David, 100

González, Justo, 131

Goodie Mob, 2

Gregory of Nyssa, 142, 151

Green, Joel, 78, 79, 85

Haas, G. H., 145, 147

Häkkinen, Sakari, 56

Hall, Stuart, 142

Hamilton, Victor, 100, 150, 150

Hammon, Jupiter, 171-72

Hammond, James Henry, 146

Harrill, J. A., 53

Hays, Richard, 28

Hoehner, H. W., 54, 56

Holland, Tom, 142, 151

Hooks, Bell, 182

Horsley, Richard, 58

Hossfeld, Frank-Lothar, 124

Hoyt, Thomas, Jr., 39

Ingraham, Christopher, 26

Isichei, Elizabeth, 97-98

Jackson, Mahalia, 2

Jau, Francis le, 169

Jennings, Willie James, 121, 124

Jensen, Morten Hørning, 54

Jewett, Robert, 34

Johnson, Luke Timothy, 77-78

Jones, Absalom, 75-76

Jones-Warsaw, Koala, 181

Julian (Missionary to Nubia), 98

Junior, Nyasha, 181, 181

Keck, Leander, 30

Keener, Craig, 59

Kendi, Ibram, 94

King, Martin Luther, Jr., 48-51, 62, 65, 112-13, 121

Knight, George W., III, 53

Lampe, Peter, 38

Lewis, Lloyd A., 153

Lincoln, C. Eric, 174

Lohse, Edward, 61

Luz, Ulrich, 66

Mamiya, Lawrence H., 174

Marcus, Joel, 42, 56, 56

Marshall, I. Howard, 55

Martin, Clarice, 52
Martinsen, Anders, 159
Martyn, J. Louis, 59
May, Cedric, 172
McCaulley, Esau, 104-6, 114, 132
Milgrom, Jacob, 146, 147
Mitchell, Margaret M., 152
Morris, Leon, 34, 64, 65
Morrison, Craig, 103
Mother Pollard, 47
Motyer, J. Alec, 110
Mounce, Robert, 63
Murphy, Larry, 146
Nas, 133
Noel, James, 152, 153, 155
Noll, Mark, 10
Nolland, John, 43, 75
Novenson, Matthew, 132
Oliver, Isaac, 75
O'Neale, Sondra, 172
OutKast, 2, 4, 5
Pao, David W., 154
Parson, Michael, 110
Payne, Daniel Alexander, 63, 83

Pennington, James W. C., 137, 138-39, 143, 145, 162-63
Perkins, Pheme, 37, 37
Powery, Luke, 107, 108
Prewitt, J.F., 108
Propp, William H. C., 150
Raboteau, Albert J., 170
Rae, Issa, 13, 15
Riesner, R., 85
Roberts, J. Doetis, 184
Rooker, Mark, 146
Rosner, Brian, 158
Rowe, C. Kavin, 90
Sanders, Cheryl, 182
Sarna, Nahum, 150, 150, 151
Sernett, Milton, 81, 83, 171
Shore, Mary Hinkle, 153
Simmons, Martha, 75-76
Simmons, William, 174-75
Simone, Nina, 25
Smith, Mitzi, 153, 169, 176, 180-83
Socrates, 133
Southern, Pat, 36
St. Clair, Raquel, 181
Stein, Robert H., 56

Stott, John, 68
Strelan, Rick, 75
Stuart, Douglas, 102
Stubbs, Monya, 30, 33
Talbert, Charles, 59
Tertullian of Carthage, 97
Thiselton, Anthony, 114
Thomas, Frank, 75-76
Thurman, Howard, 17-18, 80
Tiroyabone, Obusitswe Kingsley, 152, 155-56
Towner, Philip, 160
Townes, Emilie M., 182
Turner, Nat, 172
Walker, Alice, 181
Ware, Frederick, 181
Watts, John D. W., 58
Webb, William, 159
Weems, Renita, 97, 176, 182
Wheatley, Phyllis, 171-72
Whelchel, H. L., 170-72
White, Leon, 176
Williams, D. K., 152-53, 155
Wimbush, Vincent, 169, 181
Wright, N. T., 58, 160
Zenger, Erich, 124

SCRIPTURE INDEX

OLD TESTAMENT

Genesis
9:20-27, *100*
10:1-32, *99*
11, *99*
12:1-3, *99, 103*
12:3, *105*
13, *100*
15:17-18, *104*
17, *100*
18:25, *25*
22, *100*
28, *100*
35, *100*
39:8-9, *161*
41:40, *101*
48, *100*
48:3-5, *101*
50:19-21, *129*

Exodus
2:1-10, *180*
2:11-15, *33*
3:1-22, *33*
3:7-8, *137*
3:7-10, *32, 143*
12:38, *102*
19–40, *150*
21:20-21, *149*
21:26-27, *150*
32:1-17, *90*

Leviticus
10:10-11, *79*
11:45, *143*
23–27, *146, 147*
25:39-46, *146*

Deuteronomy
7:8, *143*
15:12-15, *145*
21:10–34:12, *149*
23:15-16, *148*

24:1-4, *140*
24:17, *143*

2 Samuel
7:14, *103*

Psalms
3, *124*
69:23-24, *123*
72, *103, 104, 106*
72:1-4, *90, 104*
72:8, *104*
101–150, *124*
109, *123*
109:7-10, *123*
137, *123, 124, 125, 126, 127, 128, 129, 133*
137:1-2, *124*
137:3-5, *125*
137:7-9, *126*

Song of Solomon
1:5, *96*

Isaiah
1:4, *58*
1:17, *58*
2:1-5, *100*
2:2-4, *147*
2:2-5, *128*
2:3, *147*
5:7-8, *179*
5:8, *57*
5:11, *179*
9:6-7, *67*
9:7, *67, 68*
11:1-9, *68*
11:1-10, *128, 129*
11:6-9, *68*
13:11, *63*
14:4-6, *63*
14:13, *63*
25:6, *147*

34–66, *58*
40, *82*
40–66, *92*
42:9, *60*
49:6, *128*
51:4, *148*
51:9-10, *88*
52:10-12, *88*
52:11-12, *109*
52:13–53:12, *88, 109*
53, *109, 110*
58:1-6, *94*
58:3, *92*
58:5-6, *92*
58:6, *91, 92, 94*
61:1, *91, 92, 93*
61:1-2, *58*
65:13, *60*
65:17, *60*

Jeremiah
8:20, *81*

Ezekiel
37:1-14, *83*

Daniel
2:20-21, *33*
7:1-28, *32*

Habakkuk
2:1-4, *62*

Zechariah
8:20-23, *128*

NEW TESTAMENT

Matthew
1–7, *66*
1:1, *105*
1:18-19, *85*

5–7, *64*
5:4, *65*
5:6, *65*
5:9, *50, 67*
10:28, *30*
10:38, *107*
16:21, *140*
16:24, *107*
19:3-8, *140*
22:31-32, *83*
23:32, *83*
26:52, *34*
27:27-30, *44*
28:18-20, *54*

Mark
1–8, *56*
10:47, *105*

Luke
1, *43, 75*
1–2, *54*
1:1, *76*
1:1-4, *76, 77*
1:1–9:50, *43, 75*
1:5, *80*
1:35, *85*
1:38, *107*
1:50, *87*
1:51, *87*
1:52-53, *71*
1:52-54, *87*
1:66, *83*
1:68-79, *42*
1:71-79, *132*
2:25, *82*
2:33-35, *89*
3:1-6, *42*
3:4-6, *42*
3:10-14, *80*
3:14, *43*
3:22, *90*
4:1-13, *90*
4:14-21, *58*

7:19, *132*
13:31, *54*
13:32, *50*
13:32-33, *56*
13:33, *57*
23:34, *133*
24:25-27, *140*

John
1:14, *85*
8:56, *105*

Acts
1:8, *108*
8:4, *108*
8:26, *108*
8:32-33, *109*
13:1-3, *112*
15, *75*
17:26, *171*
26:8, *86*

Romans
3:23, *132*
4:25, *59, 109, 131,*
  180
5:5, *164*
8:17, *107*
8:32, *59, 109*
9:16, *51*
9:17, *32, 45*
11:13, *114*

13, *30, 32, 51*
13:1-2, *29, 30, 32,*
  33, 34, 51
13:1-7, *29, 30, 40,*
  50, 51, 70
13:3-4, *34, 35, 39,*
  43
13:4, *40*
15:8, *105*
15:12, *105*
16:13, *108*

1 Corinthians
1:18, *118*
1:18-31, *154*
1:26-29, *111*
1:28, *93*
7:17, *157*
7:21, *158*
7:21-23, *158*
7:21-24, *152, 157,*
  159
9:20-23, *114*
15:12-19, *134*

2 Corinthians
4:13, *1*

Galatians
1:3-5, *59*
1:4, *50, 109*
2:20, *109, 131*

3:16, *100*
3:19-24, *141*
3:21, *141*
3:28, *18, 61, 113, 114*
4:4-5, *76*
4:4-7, *76*
4:16, *47*
4:19, *107*

Ephesians
1:21, *59*

Philippians
2:6-8, *130*
2:15-21, *154*

Colossians
1:13, *61*

1 Timothy
1:8-11, *52, 53, 70*
1:10, *53*
2:1-4, *50, 51, 52, 64,*
  70
2:1-7, *69*
6:1-2, *138*
6:1-3, *19, 139, 152,*
  159, 160, 161, 184

Philemon
1:1, *152*
1:8-9, *154*

1:9, *152*
1:10, *152*
1:11, *153*
1:12, *152*
1:23, *152*

James
1:27, *133*
2:5, *93*

1 John
1:3-4, *106*

Revelation
1:1-20, *114*
2:1–3:22, *114*
4:1-11, *115*
5:1-4, *115*
5:5, *105, 115*
6–8, *115*
6:10, *135*
7:9, *135*
7:9-10, *115*
17–22, *63*
18, *50, 62, 63*
18:2, *62*
18:21-24, *135*
18:24, *63*
19:11-14, *129*
21:3-4, *142*